Contents

Foreword by Tony Cline   **3**

1   Introduction   **5**

    The aims of this book   5
    What is nurture work?   6
    Nurture groups are about learning and teaching   6
    Update of previous guidelines   6
    The authors   8

**2   The nurture group principles and
the principles in practice**   **9**

    Children's learning is understood developmentally   10
    The classroom offers a safe base   11
    The importance of nurture for the development of self-esteem 12
    Language as a vital means of communication   13
    It is understood that all behaviour is communication   14
    The importance of transitions in children's lives is understood 15

3   Inclusion   **17**

    The National Curriculum   17
    The National Curriculum: general teaching requirements   18
    The National Curriculum: three principles of inclusion   18
    What do these three principles mean for nurture group teachers? 19

4   Curriculum planning overview   **27**

    Nurture Curriculum or nurturing curriculum?   28
    The Nurture Curriculum   29

Nurture Curriculum and the Boxall Profile | 30
Nurturing Curriculum | 30
National Curriculum | 31
Insights from neuroscience | 32

5   Organising for teaching and learning   35

Full-time nurture groups | 35
Part-time nurture groups | 36
Cross-phase groups | 36
Working in partnership with teaching assistants, specialist teachers
and class teachers | 36
Daily routines and rituals | 37
Practicalities of running a nurture group within a mainstream school | 37
Reintegration | 39
Nurture group environment and resources | 40

6   Language and communication in the nurture group   41

Asessment for learning | 43
Early learning goals for communication and language | 44
Early goals for literacy | 45
Supporting communication | 46
Developing language in the nurture group | 48

7   Creative Development   53

The importance of creativity and imagination | 53
Creating an environment in the nurture group where creativity and
imagination can flourish | 55
Knowledge, skills and understanding | 56
Exploring media and material | 57
Imagination | 60
Responding to experience | 64
Express and communicate their ideas, thoughts and feelings | 68

**8   Monitoring, assessment, record keeping,
       reporting and accountability   71**

Appendices   77

Bibliography   93

Index   96

Foreword

When Sylvia Lucas and others set up the first nurture groups in Hackney in the late 60s, the world of primary education was very different from what it is now. Few educationists were persuaded that a school-based regime would give the help that was needed for children with emotional and behaviour difficulties to work towards re-integration in their mainstream primary classes in urban areas. But with Marjorie Boxall's leadership and tentative but reliable support from the Inner London Education Authority, the first experimental groups were established in a very small number of East London primary schools. The Nurture Group model emphasised the children's capacity for growth and for learning, but perhaps inevitably the first priority in that period was to evolve effective strategies for addressing their emotional and social needs. With hindsight it is possible to recognise that many of the features of the approach are characteristic of what is now most highly valued in strategies for educational inclusion. But the primary curriculum and primary pedagogy has evolved significantly over the intervening period with particularly dramatic developments in the last decade. The authors of this text have chosen a very good time to pull together the threads of curriculum change and examine how nurture group principles may apply in the current context. The book they have produced provides a guide for this purpose which is detailed, practical and intellectually coherent. There are not many books on the primary curriculum and inclusion that can make that claim.

Tony Cline
Co-Director of the CPD Doctorate in Educational Psychology, UCL
& Professor of Educational Psychology, University of Luton
May 2006

1
Introduction

The aims of this book

This book is a hands-on working tool for nurture group teachers and class teachers working in nurturing schools. It is not intended to be the last word on the subject of the curriculum for nurture groups and it is fully expected that there will be further development in the near future.

Our belief is that a nurturing curriculum will enable all children to access the National Curriculum at a level appropriate to their presenting needs.

Recent government initiatives have highlighted the importance of inclusion for all children through identifying the expected outcomes regarding their health, safety, enjoyment and achievement, positive contribution and achievement of economic well being – that is *Every Child Matters: Change for Children* (2004). The book aims to help realise this through:

- clarifying the essential elements of a curriculum for nurture groups and nurturing classes;

- supporting nurture group teachers in devising a Nurture Curriculum for children who are at the pre-foundation stage in one or more areas of their development, based on their assessment using the Boxall Profile;

- supporting nurture group teachers in planning and assessing the National Curriculum to meet the learning needs of a group of children with a range of abilities who need a Nurturing Curriculum;

- supporting class teachers in planning the National Curriculum for children in a nurturing classroom;

and

- demonstrating how aspects of nurture group theory and practice link together.

What is nurture-work?

Adults – teachers, classroom assistants, learning mentors – who are drawn to work in nurture groups or nurturing classes are usually experienced classroom practitioners who have an intuitive understanding of children's developmental needs, which makes them able to make relationships at the appropriate level. This was Marjorie Boxall's insight and inspiration which led to setting up the first nurture groups and still provides 'the basis of nurture-work' as she describes:

> *Nurture-work is based on the observation that everyone developmentally ahead of the baby and toddler seems biologically programmed into relating to them in a developmentally appropriate way.*

(Boxall, 2002, p. 4).

This is the essence of our work. Our professional training and academic study whether as educational psychologists, head teachers, nurture group teachers, class teachers or teaching assistants will inform and deepen our understanding but we must never lose sight of the fact that we have within us the potential to respond to the needs of the children we meet. This insight, while initially intuitive, is now supported by the findings of neuroscience. (Gerhardt, 2004).

Nurture groups are about learning and teaching

Nurture groups are part of mainstream school provision. Learning and teaching – *the curriculum* – is at the heart of all that we do. Nurture groups are about 'growth not pathology' (Boxall, 2002, p. 10). They differ from most other forms of intervention for children who are vulnerable to social, emotional and behavioural difficulties by an emphasis on the curriculum, what children can know, understand, and do. Where learning is being hindered we seek to understand what is preventing development and progress rather than focus on the problems.

Update of previous guidelines

The first published nurture group curriculum, *Curriculum Guidelines for Nurture Groups 2001* was produced by the staff of the Enfield nurture groups following consultation and agreement with the head teachers of the Enfield schools, the Schools Psychological Service and the LEA (AWCEBD, 2001).

The education agenda has continued to move forward rapidly over the past five years with the recognition of the *Curriculum Guidance for the Foundation Stage* (QCA/DfEE, 2000) as an essential element of the National Curriculum and therefore now statutory provision, *Excellence and Enjoyment: A Strategy for Primary Schools* (DfES, 2003, now referred to as the Primary National Strategy), and the effects of the implementation of the *Special Educational*

Needs and Disabilities Act 2001. We have also seen the revised Code of Practice and publication of the Wave 3 materials (DfES, 11/2002, p. 3) including P scales and, most recently, *Every Child Matters*. All these initiatives are having a profound effect on learning and teaching and need to be taken into account in teachers' assessment, planning and organisation for teaching – hence the need for this new guidance.

As schools are encouraged to move away from the narrower and more prescriptive approach to the National Curriculum they may feel freer to provide a curriculum that more directly meets the needs of children in nurture groups but without losing sight of the benefits to children of the National Curriculum and their entitlement to it.

Some of the strengths and features of the much earlier Nurture Curriculum from pre-National Curriculum days, particularly for developmental stages 0 to 3 years which was overshadowed by the National Curriculum, may again be appropriately included along with the more rigorous approach to teaching and learning of the present day although it has to be recognised that teachers who have trained more recently may not find it a simple matter to relinquish the tight structures they have come to rely on.

Nurture groups too have moved on since 2001. A National Network is now firmly established with a Director, Executive and a Training Officer to oversee training in three Universities and a growing number of LAs.

These new guidelines are intended to provide up-to-date material to support nurture group teachers in their curriculum planning, taking into account all these recent initiatives. They are also intended to deepen teachers' understanding of the rationale and principles for nurture groups that underpin the approach, enabling teachers developing or already working in one of the newer variations of nurture group provision to approach curriculum planning with confidence. The rapid development in nurture group training means that we now have a very competent and well-trained work force in nurture groups at post graduate level and it is hoped that the guidelines will also be of use to them as they extend their influence more widely in the education world and they themselves contribute to training.

What are nurture groups?

They are classes of between eight and 12 children, usually in a mainstream primary school, supported by the whole staff group and by parents. Nurture groups always have two members of staff. The children spend a substantial part of each week in the group but remain part of their mainstream class, joining the other children daily for planned activities.

(The Nurture group Network, *Helping children to succeed*, p. 3)

The authors

The authors have extensive experience in primary education in the classroom, in school leadership and management, in higher education and Continuing Professional Development (CPD).

Sylvia Lucas is a former nurture group teacher. She set up one of the first nurture groups in Hackney and continued to work closely with Marjorie Boxall, the originator of nurture groups, until Marjorie's death in September 2004. She has been head teacher of four primary schools in east London and is now working in Initial Teacher Education (ITE) at the Institute of Education University of London in the school of Early Childhood and Primary Education. She is responsible for setting up and starting the course 'The Theory and Practice of Nurture Groups' at the Institute of Education and now teaches alongside Kim on it. She also undertakes a range of consultancy in primary practice and school leadership.

Kim Insley has taken on responsibility from Sylvia for the course 'The Theory and Practice of Nurture Groups' at the Institute of Education where she is also a Cohort Leader on the Open Learning Part-time Primary PGCE, visiting and observing practice in a diversity of schools. She has researched music education in primary schools, focusing on the practice of the non-specialist class teacher. Her work has led her to believe that music education has an important part to play in developing the vulnerable children who will be in a nurture group, as well as those who are not in nurture groups.

Gill Buckland has worked in the field of primary education for over 25 years. Since 2000 she has developed and co-ordinated the EYSI (Early Years Social Inclusion) service in Enfield. She has been the liaison and training consultant for the Enfield Nurture Groups since 2000 and has built up a support network, resource base and training programme that ensures that the number of groups in Enfield will be able to grow year on year. Gill also contributes to the course on the theory and practice of nurture groups at the Institute of Education.

2

Nurture group principles and the principles in practice

The Nurture Group Network's six principles sum up nurture group practice and theory. They underpin the context, organisation and curriculum.

1   Children's learning is understood developmentally

2   The classroom offers a safe base

3   The importance of nurture for the development of self-esteem

4   Language as a vital means of communication

5   All behaviour is communication

6   The importance of transitions in children's lives

The curriculum in nurture groups and nurturing classes takes account of these principles in all aspects of assessment, planning and record keeping. Furthermore, the principles are evident in whole school policies so informing practice at school, class and individual levels, and in the variety of settings children might find themselves in – the dining hall, the school office, the playground as well as the classroom.

> **The Nurture Curriculum is embedded in the Nurture Group Principles**

1. Children's learning is understood developmentally

The nurture group teacher ensures that:

- there are opportunities for Personal, Social and Emotional Development beginning at the earliest levels of play, communication, language and literacy in close proximity to the adults.

- there is support for fine and gross motor development and coordination.

- there are basic experiences which are practitioner selected and directed.

- the developmental aspects of every situation are emphasised.

- children's play enables development through clear stages: sensory, experimentation, repetition, investigation and exploration.

- co-operative play is encouraged, but not expected and it is introduced in a planned and systematic way.

- national requirements and school policy are met at the appropriate level for each child within the overall nurture context.

2. The classroom offers a safe base

The nurture group teacher ensures that:

- the organisation and management of the nurture classroom are integral to the curriculum and are understood as critical to the context for learning and teaching.

- an explicit Nurture Curriculum is provided for those children who have very early developmental needs.

- in working closely with the nurture group assistant (NGA) a trusting relationship is established which offers reassurance, constancy, interest and commitment. Together they model constructive relationships and interaction.

- a domestic setting with food, comfort and consistent care and support is provided to facilitate emotional and physical attachment.

- the day is structured so that it is predictable, establishes routines and emphasises order and repetition.

- clear boundaries – both physical and emotional – are set and maintained.

- practitioners engage with the children in everyday routines – tidying up, sorting, putting away – with helpful, uncritical adult reminders.

- everyone recognises and respects the child's expression of need for play and work space.

3. The importance of nurture for the development of self-esteem

The nurture group teacher ensures that:

- practitioners value children as individuals and work to establish a close relationship with each child as the first priority.

- children are called by their names, are noticed and everyone shows pleasure in the children's achievements.

- small achievements are praised in a diversity of ways, including non-verbal such as smiling and nodding, and remembers that for children the best reward is the sense of genuine achievement.

- practitioners establish and maintain eye contact; use facial expression and vary their tone of voice, deliberately exaggerating if necessary.

- practitioners engage in and enjoy reciprocal, shared activities such as play, having meals, sharing books and reading aloud together.

- practitioners allow time for engaging in remembering and talking about events and feelings.

- music is used to establish relationships through expecting practitioners to sing with children and play finger and body games and songs.

- practitioners listen to, anticipate and are responsive to children's needs.

4. Language as a vital means of communication

The nurture group teacher ensures that:

- the crucial importance of early communication and language is understood.

- language is assessed and developed in all aspects of the curriculum at the appropriate level for the child.

- there is time and opportunity for children to express and explore the stages of language development.

- provision is made, where necessary, for additional support for children with speech and language delay or difficulties.

- practitioners maintain a verbal commentary to activities while working and playing with the children so that they make connections between the action and the language.

- practitioners use every opportunity for extended conversations, recalling and planning for tomorrow.

- opportunities are provided for imaginative play which is encouraged; practitioners model by playing 'with' for mutual enjoyment and shared learning.

- practitioners share feelings and satisfaction, and put feelings into words both with children and other adults in the classroom.

5. It is understood that all behaviour is communication

The nurture group teacher ensures that:

- practitioners relate intuitively to the child in a developmentally appropriate way: cradling, holding, rocking; sensory exploration.

- practitioners understand the importance and significance of non-verbal communication and respond appropriately.

- practitioners understand that physical contact may be communication.

- a variety of strategies is developed such as distraction and humour (but not sarcasm) in order to respond to behaviour.

- practitioners respond to undesirable behaviour firmly but not punitively, they are not discouraged or provoked.

- children will sense that as their behaviour is understood rather than judged, difficult situations may be diffused.

- practitioners observe and record objectively without making judgements but with growing understanding of developmental levels.

- the Boxall Profile is used regularly for assessment and that practitioners base Individual Education Plans (IEPs) and Individual Learning Plans (ILPs) on the needs identified in the Developmental Strands as well as National Curriculum levels.

6. The importance of transitions in children's lives is understood

The nurture group teacher ensures that:

- a simple and manageable routine is provided which is slow moving and has a clear time structure so establishing a secure base.

- school transitions between lessons and sessions are given time and prepared for, so supporting and affirming.

- children are prepared for changes in routine, such as teacher absence and visitors, so establishing clear procedures known to the children beforehand.

- simple changes are introduced to the routine and environment. These are prepared for in detail, for example off site visits in the local area to accustom children to change.

- practitioners allow opportunity for children to talk about and comment on 'out of school transitions', they involve parents wherever and as much as possible.

- the school community understands that children may be unable to sustain achievements and may need support during times of stress.

- practitioners make use of transitional objects to help a child separate.

- in the event of bereavement a nurture child is supported and practitioners work alongside the school's protocol for bereavement and family trauma.

- reintegration is planned for and managed to ensure optimum success.

3

Inclusion

*All children should have access to an appropriate education that affords
them the opportunity to achieve their personal potential.*

(DfES, 2001)

Schools with nurture groups are inclusive. Working in the school with a nurture group means that there is recognition of what inclusion means. All staff work towards children's full inclusion into mainstream classes. Children are therefore registered with their mainstream class and stay on that class's register while they are in the nurture group. Class teachers are still responsible for the children's progress so planning in both the nurture group and base classes must be collaborative. However, the curriculum in the nurture group must be suitable for the children so that it meets those children's needs – this is inclusion.

The National Curriculum

The National Curriculum, which now includes the *Curriculum Guidance for the Foundation Stage*, is statutory and is an entitlement for all children.

The introductory chapters of *The National Curriculum Handbook for Primary Teachers in England* (DfEE/QCA, 1999) and *Curriculum Guidance for the Foundation Stage* (QCA, 2000) are often overlooked but they are essential references for nurture group teachers and they need to be read carefully. These publications are written with the child at the centre of the process but teachers often consider the curriculum to be the driving factor.

Similarly, the National Strategies for Literacy and Numeracy considered within the Primary National Strategy, *Excellence and Enjoyment* (DfES, 2003) should be read and understood in this context. These ideas are revisited later in this book in Chapter 4: Curriculum Planning Overview.

The National Curriculum: general teaching requirements (pp. 30–40)

The introduction to the National Curriculum document is particularly helpful, especially the first chapter entitled 'Inclusion: providing learning opportunities for all pupils'.

> *The National Curriculum is the starting point for planning a school curriculum that meets the needs of individuals and groups of pupils.* This statutory inclusion statement on providing effective learning opportunities for all pupils *outlines how teachers can modify, as necessary, the National Curriculum programmes of study to provide all pupils with relevant and appropriately challenging work at each key stage.*

> (DfEE/QCA, 1999, p. 30, emphasis added)

This identifies one way in which schools can work in an inclusive way – by using the (now extended) curriculum so that children can work at the level they are at, rather than the level teachers, parents, or even government, might perceive them to be because of their chronological age. It now means it is feasible to have a nine-year-old working within the foundation stage curriculum without having to 'disapply' or 'exclude' a child.

What nurture groups do further is support children's needs for learning outside this national curriculum so enabling their access to it. The first principle recognises children's learning as developmental. But where does that development start? In order to ensure children can access the curriculum appropriate for their chronological age, their earlier developmental needs must have been met. For some children, missing out on earlier development means they cannot learn appropriately and are therefore 'excluded' from the curriculum.

The National Curriculum: three principles for inclusion (p. 30)

All teachers, in planning and teaching the National Curriculum, are required to have 'due regard' to these three principles.

A   Setting suitable learning challenges

B   Responding to pupils' diverse learning needs

C   Overcoming potential barriers to learning and assessment for individuals and groups of pupils

What do these three principles mean for nurture group teachers?

In order to explore these three principles further it is necessary to make reference first to the nurture group principles. All six principles map onto these three, but will apply in different ways to each.

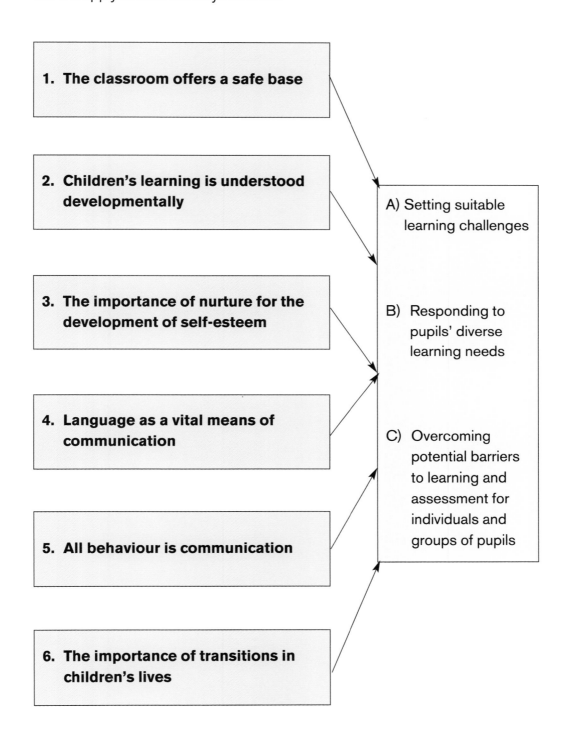

1. The classroom offers a safe base

2. Children's learning is understood developmentally

3. The importance of nurture for the development of self-esteem

4. Language as a vital means of communication

5. All behaviour is communication

6. The importance of transitions in children's lives

A) Setting suitable learning challenges

B) Responding to pupils' diverse learning needs

C) Overcoming potential barriers to learning and assessment for individuals and groups of pupils

A. Setting suitable learning challenges

Aspect	What this really means
The content of the work provided is at the appropriate developmental level.	Matching the work to the children's needs rather than teaching what they should be doing at their age.
The response/outcome expected is at the appropriate developmental level.	Children need to respond to their learning as they wish, for example a practical activity such as role play. Similarly the teacher should plan for responses that reflect the children's needs.
The organisation is at the appropriate developmental level.	Children may need to work and play in a solitary way; collaborative group work may not be appropriate; individuals need time to work through their own ideas.
Gaps in learning resulting from missed or interrupted early experience are recognised and provided for.	This is the Nurture Curriculum. Use P scales and careful analysis of the Developmental Strands of the Boxall Profile (AWCEBD 1998) to identify needs.
The National Curriculum programmes of study are used as a context for meeting other earlier learning needs, particularly in personal, social and emotional development but also early language, communication, cognitive and concept development if necessary.	The essential basic skills of learning such as the ability to listen, to wait, to choose, to share, to concentrate for a reasonable (age-appropriate) period and to persist cannot be assumed. They need to be planned for and taught explicitly.
Attainment may be age appropriate or even exceed expected levels in some areas but be significantly below in others.	Planning must take this into account and needs to be carefully differentiated across subject areas and areas of learning to allow for unevenness in development.

The nurture group environment, organisation and routines are in themselves a proven effective learning environment for children who are vulnerable to social, emotional and behavioural difficulties. They should never be disrupted without very good reason. All the nurturing activities, routines and rituals, for example breakfast, group carpet times, opportunities for solitary and small group play at a pre-school level are intended to secure the children's motivation and build up their concentration.

The processes of the group are as powerful a teaching and learning medium as the more obvious curriculum work. In many instances the process or organisation is, in fact, the curriculum.

Case study

Colin is 5 years old. He is big for his age and physically robust. In the nursery class he was very unresponsive and did not engage with children or adults. He appeared sullen, lacking interest and curiosity in any activity offered to him. He was passively biddable but his teachers felt that he was depressed rather than cooperative. His scores on the Developmental Strands of Boxall Profile and his base line assessment were very low. He showed no improvement after a term in the reception class and was admitted to the nurture group.

The teacher continues to work with him at a foundation stage level in language and communication, mathematical development and knowledge and understanding of the world. He needs KS1 level PE opportunities to use his energy and to develop his control and coordination. But she also notices from her observations that he avoids normal physical contact and eye contact. In fact his facial expression does not change and he fails to smile. Encouraging him to smile becomes the most important target and she and the NGA make frequent, brief opportunities during the day for one-to-one play at a 0–3 month level (see Appendix 1, pp. 77–79).

B. Responding to pupils' diverse learning needs

Aspect	What this really means
Expectations of the children should be as high as those in the mainstream class.	Difficulties of behaviour are not an excuse for low standards of achievement.
All children should have the opportunity to achieve.	The ability to read is crucial to self-esteem. The nurture group is not only a therapeutic quiet place where children come and play.
Children's previous experiences will influence the way in which they learn.	Children who have experienced failure will bring this with them, and until they start to achieve they will still expect to fail. They may not even make the effort to achieve or succeed.
Their interests and strengths may be out of the ordinary.	Children who have not experienced structure may not make the connections between their learning, but still demonstrate extraordinary knowledge rather than understanding.
Approaches to teaching and learning will need to be carefully planned to enable all children to take part in lessons fully and effectively.	Differentiation will be individual so planned activities and work needs to be open ended and not require a closed response.
Equal opportunities awareness is essential.	Knowing about your children's cultural background, their families' expectations and how they might respond ensures that the children's access to the learning being offered is open.

Children in nurture groups may range from those who are very passive and non-communicative to those who are aggressive and demanding. It is important to make sure that selection for the group is balanced along this continuum. This may mean delaying entry to the nurture group for some children.

When organising the nurture group day these diversities will need to be catered for, although the basic organisation as discussed in A above will not change radically as all children will benefit. The activities planned, and practitioners' interactions will be in response to children's needs, but still within the recognised structure of the nurture group day.

Case study

Rosina is a refugee and has a limited grasp of English although she appears to understand more than she can speak. She is nine years old but is very withdrawn and so unhappy in the classroom that she is unable to work. In the playground she does not engage with other children of her age but seeks out much younger children from Reception and Year 1 to play with. She seems to enjoy caring for them and has followed them back to class to play in the role play areas, usually taking on a domestic role – cooking, sweeping, washing.

The nurture group is mainly for Key Stage 1 children but Rosina is happy to join them. She settled very quickly into the homely atmosphere of the group. The focus on language games and activities and the continuous running commentary by the teacher and NGA on what is happening has helped her understanding of English but her speech continues to be almost non existent. A recent hearing test during a routine medical examination has revealed that Rosina has badly damaged ear drums and is seriously hearing impaired. She also has suffered extensive burns. She is now able to have support from the hearing impaired service who will work with an EAL teacher with her. The safety and security of the nurture group are providing much needed stability and slowly she is beginning to develop an interest in what is happening around her.

C. Overcoming potential barriers to learning and assessment for individuals and groups of pupils

Aspect	What this really means
Helping with communication, language and literacy.	Knowing, recognising and responding to the early stages of language development; the importance of reciprocity of language for building attachment and trust; using texts that children can read and understand and allowing time for repetition and assimilation; using ICT.
Using a wide range of material and resources that children can access through the use of all available senses and experiences.	Giving first hand experience wherever possible; participating in simple everyday activities, pre-school play activities, role play. Simple off-site visits and getting to know the local environment.
Full participation in learning and physical and practical activities.	This will be achieved through support from the nurture teacher and nurture group assistant, modifying tasks and the environment to provide nurturing experiences, for example allowing for floor space so that children can spread out and find their own space.
Helping children to manage their behaviour and their emotions particularly trauma and stress.	This means building a parent–child relationship of trust and attachment and providing a safe and secure environment which is predictable and which enables them to build a sense of identity and to take part in learning.
Providing carefully selected activities at the appropriate developmental level.	See A and B above.
Giving positive feedback and building self-esteem.	Having a slow moving day with clear routines and rituals and avoiding unnecessary stress; allowing time for children to engage in learning and gradually to extend the range of activities and demands as their developmental stage suggests.

Aspect	What this really means
Giving particular attention to managing times of transition both in and out of school.	Allowing children to take 'security blankets' (transitional objects) with them, for example a soft toy.
Recognising that behaviour is more than what is observed.	Children might be trying to tell you something by their behaviour; might not know what is the appropriate behaviour so adults need to model it. The behaviour itself might be fully appropriate for the developmental stage so react to it as such. Work together, adults and children, to establish appropriate behaviour.
Modelling appropriate adult–adult relationships so that children are secure within the setting and supporting appropriate adult–child relationships which are dynamic and secure.	It's all right for the children to see you and your nurture group assistant laughing together, discussing, and even sometimes not agreeing! Saying sorry to a child or an adult when you have been wrong.

There may be limitless numbers of barriers in any nurture group setting but if these are seen as challenges to the teaching then they can be overcome. The children or their parents may not perceive the same barriers as you do. Often perceptions are that schools create the problem – and so they might! The first step is to recognise the challenges so that planning, the environment and approaches can be adapted to enable everyone to access the curriculum.

Of course, these same challenges may be recognised in the ordinary classroom but the class teacher has limited resources available to meet them. In order to include the children the school's response is to provide a nurture group. In the nurture group setting there is time, space and resources to better investigate and solve the challenges. Not all will be solved as there may be other provision that is needed.

Useful websites

www.literacytrust.org.uk
www.nc.uk.net/inclusion.html
www.everychildmatters.gov.uk
http://inclusion.uwe.ac.uk/csie/index launch

www.ican.org.uk
http://inclusion.ngfl.gov.uk
www.qca.org.uk/6166.html

Case study

Tom is a third child who started school as a rising five, apparently unable to communicate with adults or other children. His mother and brother and sister often spoke for him, but not to him. In the reception class he spent most of the day stood at the playground door watching for his mother to return. He displayed obsessive behaviour in rushing from the playground door to tuck in a chair every time another child left it away from the desk, but Tom always returned to the playground door.

In the nurture group he began to make an attachment and developed trust in the teacher and NGA. His early learning needs were identified and met by providing early play activities so that adults played next to him, sharing his discoveries and talking about what was happening by keeping up a running commentary. Tom was allowed to discover his voice by making noises. He began to respond to the repetition of his name and was happy looking at the adults to see what their response to his behaviour was going to be. He began to delight in being smiled at. The focus of language and communication was a priority within the context of the relationships.

Conclusion

The nurture group is inclusive practice. Children are registered with their main class and return there for registration. Sometimes sessions such as PE and music may take place with the registration class. With the development of the Primary National Strategy and themed approaches to planning, the nurture group will be situated at the centre of the school – it becomes the heart of the school.

> *If nurture groups are to contribute to the sort of inclusion that benefits the child, it is important, as has been frequently said, that the group is a highly regarded, well-understood, integral part of the school. [. . .] If nurture groups are set up in the way recommended, they are not only 'inclusive' in the best meaning of the term, they also contribute to the inclusive ethos of the whole school.*
>
> (Bennathan and Boxall, 2000)

4

Curriculum planning overview

Inclusion begins with the whole school, but curriculum planning in the nurture group begins with the children. In considering children's needs the starting point is the Nurture Group Principles. If we adhere to these we have the framework – the nurture group – in order to see the needs of the individual. We use various assessment processes to clarify these needs. And rather than planning leading to assessment, we focus on assessment leading to planning so that the planning starts from what children can do. This process will be informed by children's Individual Education Plans (IEPs) so that an Individual Learning Plan (ILP) for each individual is developed. It is essentially positive and an assessment of what the child can do. This then highlights the next steps in individual learning. The children's ILPs inform the generic planning in the nurture group. This planning will be collaborative planning with the base class teachers. The diagram below shows how already established planning might inform the nurture group planning.

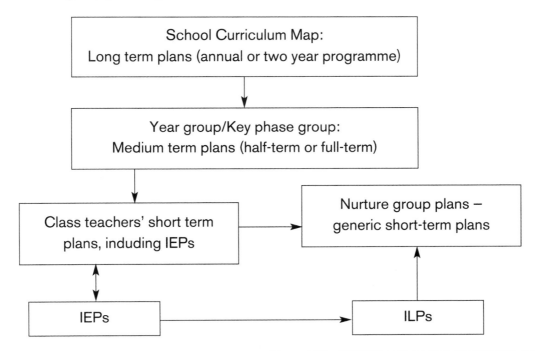

Difficulties arise when the nurture group includes children from different year groups, where different themes are informing plans. In reflecting on the vulnerable children who will be in the nurture group, it may be more appropriate to change the themes supporting the curriculum.

In considering the Nurture Group Principles, and the recognition that children in the nurture group have an optimum period of approximately four terms, it is suggested that the differentiation in the nurture group reflects three themes. At the first level is 'Myself', developing into 'The School and people in it' and then considering 'The Neighbourhood'.

Within these three themes children may visit the topics being studied in their base classes and strands from both may be incorporated into the ILP. It may be that some children are returning to their base class for some teaching – for example foundation subjects – and will therefore find the connections support their learning in both classes. In the fourth term children should revisit the first theme, so enabling them to reflect on how they have 'grown' in the nurture group.

This is a suggestion only. It is not prescribed nurture group practice, but does demonstrate the importance of the nurture group teacher's role within whole school planning. There needs to be communication with all those planning for children's needs, and the best place for the nurture group is at the centre of the school. This idea is explored further in Chapter 3: Inclusion.

Nurture Curriculum or nurturing curriculum?

Marjorie Boxall (2002) describes clearly the features of the children that she identifies as **nurture children** and others she calls **children who need nurturing**. She writes:

> Nurture children *are functioning below the age of three, and all have considerable emotional, behavioural and learning difficulties . . . these difficulties . . . all seemed related to impoverishment and loss in the first three years. It followed that an effective approach to a wide range of difficulties stemming from deprivation of many kinds was to create the world of early childhood in school and so provide a broadly based learning experience, normally gained in the first three years.*
>
> (Boxall, 2002, pp. 2 and 3)

Children who need nurturing also benefit from the nurture group although their needs are different. These children may be 'emotionally disorganised' but have had opportunities for basic learning in the earliest years. These children, Marjorie Boxall goes on to say,

. . . have some functional experience of the world about them and relevant skills, and to some extent are able to control their own behaviour and reflect on experience, but destructive and distorting experiences, and in some cases harmful separations, have interfered with their personal and social development.

(Boxall, 2002, p. 3)

In some cases, these are children who have experienced trauma as well as separation and may also be refugees or asylum seekers. It may be that children from families which are highly mobile during their early education years display aspects of poor attachment related to the school environment, although there is a recognised attachment to the family.

It follows that the learning needs of these two sub-groups of children, both commonly found in nurture groups, will be different, although there may at times be considerable overlap. To distinguish the differences in the curriculum we need to provide for the two groups we use the terms **Nurture Curriculum** for the first group and **Nurtur*ing* Curriculum** for the second group.

These curricula are not necessarily separate although they may be. They will however inter-relate as while they may address different developmental levels they both focus on the same key areas of

- personal, social and emotional development;

- communication and language;

- motor development and coordination.

The Nurture Curriculum

This covers all the learning of the earliest years (from 0–3 years) that is usually the experience of a young child in the home with a 'good enough'* parent. These experiences form the foundation for a successful early years education. They are the process as well as the outcome of a secure attachment and an appropriate response from the parent to the child's normal thrust for growth. At the time of publication aspects of the government's green paper, *Every Child Matters* are being implemented following *The Children Act 2004* and these are informing curriculum developments. Its agenda includes developing 'integrated children's services', the 'extended school day' and a 'common assessment framework', but there will still be vulnerable children who will need nurture groups.

---

* A term first used by Donald Winnicott and used as a title for CCETSW report in 1978

The fundamental processes of the nurture group as set out in the Nurture Group Principles are integral to the **Nurture Curriculum** as they are concerned with the building up of a sense of attachment and trust through a close adult/parent–child relationship and a sense of personal identity.

To achieve this quality of relationship in a school setting, these experiences or processes, require explicit teaching and need to be as carefully and systematically planned for as any other area of the curriculum. All the accepted requirements of curriculum planning apply, namely:

- assessment – Boxall Profile;
- long, medium and short term plans;
- clear learning objectives;
- evaluation and assessment.

The Nurture Curriculum and the Boxall Profile

The **Nurture Curriculum** is a generic and holistic approach to what could be seen as IEP (or LSP in some LAs) targets informed by an analysis of the child's scores on the Boxall Profile.

> While the child's developmental needs as identified by the Boxall Profile will inform the teacher's understanding of the nature of the difficulties and should ensure that provision is made at the appropriate level, any attempt to address the specific need directly would be counter productive. To take this route would not be in keeping with the underlying philosophy of nurture groups which is one of 'growth not pathology'. The 'perspective is forward looking from birth, not looking back from the present' (Boxall, 2002, p. 10).

The basis for the **Nurture Curriculum** is Marjorie Boxall's 'Earliest learning: a summary chart' (Boxall, 2002, pp. 5–9). It exemplifies this approach and is reproduced at Appendix 1, pp. 77–79.

The Nurturing Curriculum

This allows the child, who is at a later Key Stage, to revisit areas of the Foundation, Key Stage 1 and 2 Curricula that might have been missed or insufficiently experienced and that are now becoming a barrier to learning. In particular, the Personal, Social and Emotional Development area of learning may have not been sufficiently well consolidated for children with special needs in that area or especially in children who may have missed out on nursery experience. Learning to wait, to share and to choose are key skills for learning and behaviour in the mainstream classroom.

The National Curriculum

All children have an entitlement to the National Curriculum and it must be taught. It is also an essential guide to the expected age-related, learning, progress and attainment for all children and as such is an invaluable *starting* point for teachers of children with – or vulnerable to – SEN.

The DfES through the Training and Development Agency for schools (TDA) supports teachers in planning for the National Curriculum through various websites (see Bibliography). In particular the QCA schemes of work, medium and short term plans are accessed by many teachers and formulate the basis of the curriculum offered to children in school. Teachers are now able to access vast stores of lesson plan ideas and activities. Sometimes the choice is too great! However, in considering the diversity of needs of the children in their care, nurture group teachers can access these as a resource to ensure that the Programmes of Study of the National Curriculum are being covered either in the base class or in the nurture group for those areas of the curriculum where children are able to achieve at the appropriate level.

Many children in nurture groups are of at least average ability. Others may be gifted and talented and therefore able to work at levels beyond those expected at their age. An Individual Learning Plan (ILP) will include all these elements (see below) and show a wider picture for planning than the more common Individual Education Plan (IEP). IEPs are a valuable tool for tracking progress but a narrow, target-based approach tends to focus too much attention on what children cannot do. For children of average ability or above then, the National Curriculum may actually be the vehicle for teaching social, emotional and behavioural skills.

As in all nurture group work, the area of Personal, Social and Emotional education takes priority. In focussing on this, we identify *how* the children work (i.e. learning behaviour, the affective aspect). *What* they are learning (i.e. subject matter, the cognitive aspect) is important in the planning stage, but the nurture group teacher ensures that how they access this is informed by children's personal, social and emotional needs.

All children in the nurture group will have an Individualised Learning Plan developed from:

- The Nurture Curriculum: the missed experiences from the earliest years (0–3 years) i.e. pre-foundation PSED
- The Nurturing Curriculum: opportunity to revisit areas of learning from Foundation Stage or KS1 or KS2
- The National Curriculum: age appropriate levels or even above. Nurture children may also be gifted and talented

Insights from neuro-science

The work of neuroscientists in exploring emotions supports our belief, derived from empirical experience, that the nurture group approach to teaching and learning is valid.

> *Our rationality . . . is built on emotion and cannot exist without it. It is increasingly being recognised that cognitions depend on emotions.*

> (Gerhadt, 2004, p. 5)

McNeil (1999) cites Golman as proposing emotional literacy programmes to support children's academic achievement as well as their behaviour. Similarly Elinor Goldschmied (1994) has worked with children under three and focuses on brain development recognising that even these very young children can concentrate for a sustained period of time when both the learning task and the learning environment are carefully structured. Aspects of her work have informed nurture group practice since the 1970s. Importantly,

> *our emotional system drives our attention system which drives learning and memory and everything else that we do.*

> (*School Improvement Network – Research Matters*,
> No 10, Spring and Summer 1999)

Conclusion

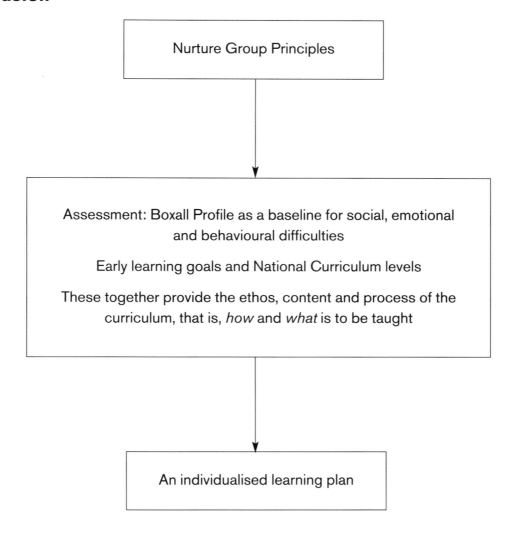

Nurture Group Principles

Assessment: Boxall Profile as a baseline for social, emotional and behavioural difficulties

Early learning goals and National Curriculum levels

These together provide the ethos, content and process of the curriculum, that is, *how* and *what* is to be taught

An individualised learning plan

Having developed the curriculum for within the nurture group it can then be evaluated by its outcomes.

By using the Boxall Profile successful learning will be recognised by an increase in the scores in the Developmental Strands while those in the Diagnostic Profile decrease.

National Curriculum levels show improving attainment and progress as a result of improving attention and motivation.

Finally, as suggested earlier, it is important that planning is shared with the class teacher who may take responsibility for the teaching of some National Curriculum elements.

Individual Learning Plan for Colin of Yellow Class, Year Group 1

	Week 1	Week 2	Week 3	Week 4	Week 5	Week 6
Nurture Curriculum *Maths* *Science* *Art* *History* *Geography* *RE* *ICT*	• Attend to the teacher • Make eye contact • Solitary play • Discovery basket					
Nurturing Curriculum *English* *Music*	**ELGs for CLL** • use words and gestures, including body language • Listen to favourite nursery rhymes, stories and songs **ELGs for CD** • Join in favourite songs • Respond to sound with body movement					
National Curriculum *PE*	**PE – KS 1** • Send and receive a ball • Is able to use a variety of means of travelling across the floor; being still; finding a space					

Source: Kim Insley and Sylvia Lucas, Sept. 2005.

5

Organising for learning and teaching

A nurture group curriculum needs to be one that is adaptable to many different situations. One booklet cannot meet the need of every individual variation but this section aims to identify the essential features that need to be considered for the more common variations.

Increasingly schools with nurture groups are finding that they are using their available resources – teachers, teaching assistants and space – in many different ways. While the Boxall group remains the classic model many versions and adaptations are occurring which hold true to the fundamental principles and can therefore claim to be authentic nurture groups.

Whatever the variation from the original model, the size of group is important. It needs to be large enough for children to learn from one another, to begin to respect one another's space and to give and take. The optimum number that allows for a reasonable range of relationships to be experienced is 10–12.

Full-time nurture groups

These are the groups that are able to follow the original Boxall model and principles most closely and will be most familiar. They offer:

- a nurture curriculum for developmental stages 0–3 years;
- a nurturing curriculum for missed or inadequately covered experiences and opportunities for consolidation of learning at foundation stage, Key Stage 1 and Key Stage 2;
- the National Curriculum and Strategies drawing on additional material, for example Wave 3 for children with SEN.

Part-time groups

Each part-time nurture group needs to devise an appropriate curriculum to meet the group or individual needs of the children taking age phase and developmental levels into account. It will have elements of the curriculum for a full-time group but responsibility for coverage will be shared with the class teacher.

The priority is the same for a full-time group, that is, for children to build a relationship of trust with the adults within a domestic setting in which they will be able to learn developmentally appropriate behaviour.

Part-time groups usually focus on the nurture and nurturing elements and a particular area of learning such as communication, language and literacy.

Cross-phase groups

The individualised nature of the nurture group curriculum with a developmental focus enables children of different age phases to be taught together provided the Nurture Group Principles can be adequately followed. The challenge of curriculum planning to meet individual needs for a wider than usual age range will be similar to that of a small school and there is useful guidance from a range of sources such as DfES and local authority web sites and www.ourschools. org.uk.

Working in partnership with nurture group assistants, specialist teachers and class teachers

Relationships are the key feature of nurture group work. The relationships between the adults and the way they collaborate is a powerful model for the children. They learn how to listen, to negotiate, and to resolve conflicts.

In addition, having two adults working together enables them to relate to the children at different developmental levels as necessary. It is the nurture group teacher who will have a special responsibility for the children in the group and will lead on curriculum matters but it is usual practice now for others to contribute their particular expertise such as EAL, hearing-impaired, etc.

Working as a team has enormous strengths: expertise is shared and enhanced, everyone benefits and the rewards far outweigh the responsibility of committing time and energy to working together.

Daily routines and rituals

These make the nurture day manageable by slowing it down and creating a calm atmosphere that can be returned to at any point during the day if it becomes necessary. Beginnings and endings of the day and sessions, collection of children from classes, group carpet sessions, breakfast, celebrations and sharing of interests – all are ritualised.

These routines and rituals are not simply organisational and class management strategies; the nurture teacher is clear about the learning that is involved and that they are an essential part of the nurture curriculum as they contain many elements of pre-foundation stage personal, social and educational development (PSED).

Other learning intentions from both the nurturing curriculum and the National Curriculum particularly in communication and language, for example extending vocabulary and ensuring understanding, might also be included when this happens naturally but these should never be allowed to distract in this context from the priorities of the nurture curriculum.

Practicalities of running a nurture group within a mainstream school

It is very important to ensure that the nurture group is an integral part of the school. If children are to fully benefit from inclusion within a nurture group it is essential to consider the following factors:

- All the staff in the school understand the aims and objectives of the nurture group and they are all supportive of the work of the nurture group staff when working with some of the most vulnerable children within the school community;

- The nurture group team works closely and supportively with other members of staff within the school;

- The nurture group staff and school have established good working relationships with other agencies that will be involved with the child and his/her family.

The whole school

If all school staff are to understand the aims and objectives of the nurture group it is important to incorporate some whole school training into the annual school plan. This training needs to include support staff and supervisory assistants. In large schools where there is a high turn over of staff this training needs to be repeated regularly.

Nurture groups flourish where there is an active commitment from the top down, through the leadership team and senior managers/governors and there exists equally positive support and understanding from the bottom up through teachers/TAs and other adults involved with children within the school setting.

Nurture groups do not have impact where there is the belief that they run as independent units.

The nurture group team and the class teacher

The nurture group team needs to set aside time to liaise routinely with other members of staff who are teaching or come into regular contact with the child. Class teachers, in particular, need to feel part of the process of the nurture group and very much valued and listened to by the nurture group staff.

Teachers often complain that they are told who is being taken into the group, or that one of their children has been selected when they feel that they have others in their class who equally need a place.

One way that may help is to make use of an observation form that can be used by the class teacher pre-Boxall profile (see Appendix 2, pp. 80–82). This form is to be completed by two adults who work with the child. The form should be completed at different times when the child is involved in different activities. The completed observation then acts as an informal profile.

On completion it can then be used as a basis for discussion with the nurture group staff. It acts as an informal tool to aid with the joint identification of children by the class teacher and nurture group staff. A Boxall profile is then completed on children who it is agreed would benefit from a place in the school's nurture group.

Once the children have been identified there is then a need for all those staff involved with the child within the school to come to an understanding of the expectations one from the other when the child goes into the nurture group (see Appendix 3, p. 83).

The use of a signed understanding can help with focusing all involved on the needs of the individual child, and how they can work together to support him/her.

Regular meetings should also be held between the appropriate members of the school senior management team such as the SENCO.

Involvement of other agencies

Schools with successful nurture groups work closely with The Educational Psychological Service, and liaise well with other involved agencies. The school's Educational Psychologist should be able to meet with the school staff on a regular basis.

One school set up a regular meeting with a social worker in order to discuss issues relating to their children's families. Another school made an arrangement for the school nurse to call into the nurture group for a few minutes whenever she was in school to chat with the children and meet parents informally. Other successful initiatives have involved community workers and Speech and Language Therapists. Often parents will come into school when they will not attend a clinic.

Reintegration

It is important that the school has a reintegration policy for children from the nurture group and all members of staff understand it. There should be good communication between the class teacher and the nurture group staff during the time that the child is in the nurture group so that a decision to start the reintegration programme should arise naturally. The SENCO should be involved in the review prior to reintegration.

The reintegration programme will be different for each child. Some schools take several weeks or even months over the process. The child might start by attending one session per week in the mainstream class and this would be for a curriculum area in which he/she could succeed. After three or four weeks another session could be added so that the child is slowly increasing his/her time in the mainstream class. The class teacher and nurture group teacher will also need to discuss the programme with the child's parent or carer. It is important to remember that there will probably be set backs and the programme should be flexible. It is also important that the child is involved in the process.

It is sometimes useful to develop a profile (see Appendix 4, pp. 84–89) for assessing progression towards reintegration and readiness to start the process. This profile can be completed when discussing the child with class teacher and SENCO. The class teacher and nurture group teacher would then be able to set targets for the child which are achievable and realistic. The Boxall Profile would be used, however, to assess the child formally.

At reintegration it is important to consider how the child will manage the full-time curriculum. New targets need to be discussed with the child in a way that recognises his/her achievements, this will ensure that the child's self esteem continues to improve. Eventually the child will effect a smooth transition to his/her mainstream class while retaining social links with the nurture group.

Nurture group environment and resources

In an ideal world a nurture group will have:

- a kitchen area with sink, cupboards, cooker, fridge, etc.;
- a role play area; dressing up clothes;
- easy furniture – sofas and chairs to provide area where children and staff can be in a relaxed, informal atmosphere;
- a dining table with adequate seating for group and staff to eat together;
- equipment appropriate for curriculum but linked to early child development and foundation stage;
- basic classroom furniture – storage essential;
- a book area with cushions;
- a large mirror – you may need to be sensitive to cultural/ faith issues;
- display boards;
- an appropriate floor covering;
- easy access to toilets;
- easy access to outside play area.

Pictures, displays, etc. are best growing from children's interests and work, rather than being provided, so as to ensure that children have ownership and can be encouraged to value and respect their surroundings.

6

Language and communication in the nurture group

It is understood that all behaviour is communication. It follows that a significant number of children within a nurture group who are 'acting out' their feelings are communicating in the only way that they know.

These children are often confronted by a school curriculum that they do not have the necessary levels of language or communication to access or understand. For this reason alone it is necessary to build into the curriculum of the nurture groups opportunities to develop and enhance the levels of language and communication of the children.

Language as a vital means of communication. The nurture group may be the first place where links between behaviour and language happen and it is a crucial aspect of the adults' role to support this process. Understanding and planning for early language acquisition and development is the first priority in nurture group curriculum planning. Language involves both *reception* and *expression*. It is essentially reciprocal, that is, it involves a process of turn-taking.

A child who has had little or no experience of 'trusted' adult interaction, e.g. turn-taking, will not have had the opportunity to develop the necessary skills to acquire the ability to communicate. Language acquisition is partly innate and partly learned, as children interact with other people and the environment.

Language has been called the symbolisation of thought. It is a learned code, or system of rules that enables us to communicate ideas and express wants and needs. Reading, writing, gesturing and speaking are all forms of language. Language falls into two main divisions: receptive language (understanding what is said, written or signed); and, expressive language (speaking, writing or signing).

Figure 1
Language Development Pyramid

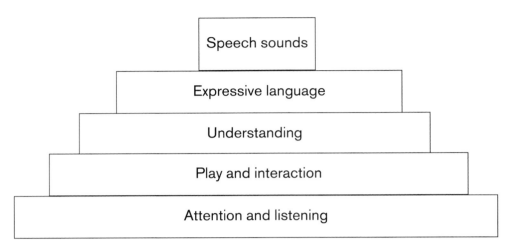

Source: Enfield/Barnet NHS

The stages of language development, shown in Figure 1, illustrate exactly why it is that vulnerable and disadvantaged children have not reached the developmental levels needed to build attachment and trust and why their communication and language skills are often functioning at the level of that of a much younger child. The frustration that they feel is frequently a trigger for inappropriate behaviour to develop.

The five building blocks of Language and Communication do not stand independently of each other; they rest on the foundation of the one below and build until speech emerges.

Babies learn very quickly to attend to the main carer and can recognise voice and mood at a very early age. They will turn their heads to focus on the adult and the beginnings of 'attachment' are formed. This is the largest block as without the dependable attention of a 'trusted adult/adults' babies soon learn to withdraw and become distressed. As a result the rest of the building blocks fail to develop properly. Play and interaction are underdeveloped and the world around them is frustratingly incomprehensible. Children learn not to respond to language, but still need to make their needs known; they resort to types of behaviour which will draw attention to their distress and emotional and behaviour difficulties develop, often alongside personal identity issues.

The nurture teacher ensures that:

- **Children's learning is understood developmentally**

- **The classroom offers a safe base**

A nurture group environment provides the ideal opportunity to develop a curriculum for language and communication that treats each child as an individual, and allows them to revisit areas that may be missing or poorly developed, that is, the nurture curriculum or nurturing curriculum.

The 'safe base' of the nurture group classroom, the fact that children are understood and managed in a developmentally appropriate way and a recognition of behaviour as communication is the perfect environment in which to develop language skills.

Assessment for Learning

There is much support for Assessment *for* Learning (rather than Assessment *of* Learning) elsewhere, both in this book and on government websites. Importantly, 80 per cent of the foundation stage is rooted in language and communication and the Early Learning Goals are valuable tools that can be used for assessing and monitoring the progress of children *of any age* within the nurture group setting. *Curriculum Guidance for the Foundation Stage* (QCA/DfEE, 2000) groups communication, language and literacy together, but for nurture children it may be necessary to consider literacy separately as this focuses on the *use* of language and communication and they may need to develop early communication and language skills before considering how they can be used.

Early learning goals for communication and language

- Interact with others, negotiating plans and activities and taking turns in conversation.

- Enjoy listening to and using spoken and written language, and readily turn to it in their play and learning.

- Sustain attentive listening, responding to what they have heard by relevant comments, questions or actions.

- Listen with enjoyment, and respond to stories, songs and other music, rhymes and poems and make up their own stories, songs, rhymes and poems.

- Extend their vocabulary, exploring the meanings and sounds of new words.

- Speak clearly and audibly with confidence and control and show awareness of the listener, for example by their use of conventions such as greetings, and saying 'please' and 'thank you'.

- Use language to imagine and recreate roles and experiences.

- Use talk to organise, sequence and clarify thinking, ideas, feelings and events.

Following on from these are the goals for literacy which are part of the foundation stage curriculum and the expectations are that by Year 1 all children will have achieved them.

Early goals for literacy

- Hear and say initial and final sounds in words, and short vowel sounds within words.

- Link sounds to letters, naming and sounding the letters of the alphabet.

- Use their phonic knowledge to write simple regular words and phonetically plausible attempts at more complex words.

- Explore and experiment with the sounds, words and texts.

- Retell narratives in the correct sequence, drawing on language patterns of stories.

- Read a range of familiar and common words and simple sentences independently.

- Know that print carries meaning and that in English is read from left to right and top to bottom.

- Show an understanding of the elements of stories, such as main character, sequence of events, and openings, and how information can be found in non-fiction texts to answer questions about where, why and how.

- Use their phonic language to write simple regular words and make phonetically plausible attempts at more complex words.

- Attempt writing for different purposes, using features of different forms such as lists, stories and instructions.

- Write their own names and other things such as labels and captions and begin to form simple sentences, sometimes using punctuation.

- Use a pencil and hold it effectively to form recognisable letters, most of which are correctly formed

Supporting communication

Within the nurture group it is possible to develop strategies which help and aid all children in developing communication. These can be broadly summarised as follows:

Gain eye contact

- Say the child's name.
- Say 'listen' and gesture to your ears.
- Be prepared to refocus the child's attention frequently.
- Be prepared to stop the child to ensure full listening and attention.

Break down verbal instructions into small steps

- Instructions should be specific to the child.
- Children with language difficulties are unable to remember or process more than one item of information at a time.

Using visual clues

This is particularly important as children with poor language and communication will have poor memory and sequencing skills. Visual clues, including signs or natural gesture, will:

- Assist children's understanding and recall.
- Situate the language.
- Enable children to focus.
- Attract children's attention.

Check understanding

It is important not to presume that children have understood questions or instructions, but to be explicit in making sure they have by reflecting on the following:

- Was the sentence too long or complex?
- Did it contain new vocabulary?
- Do any of the words used have more than one meaning?
- Are there too many concepts in one sentence? i.e. is it too complex?

Create opportunities

- reinforce language in everyday classroom activities.

- use new language in lots of different situations so that it becomes generalised rather than remaining in one context.

- Be repetitive in your teaching of new vocabulary.

Expand utterances

In much the same way as adults add to children's sentences, contextualise and elaborate the language that would be appropriate:

Child 'Look – car'
Adult 'Yes it is a car, a big, red, fast, car'

Encourage turn-taking

- Wait for children to finish before intervening or expanding the language opportunity.

- Model turn-taking in non-verbal interactions, for example playing with bricks, giving out toast.

- Create opportunities for appropriate age level turn-taking games.

- Avoid the overuse of solitary, computer games.

Developing language in the nurture group: some activities

Language is an integral part of every classroom: to maximise the development of language skills, they need to be specifically included in the learning objectives of all lessons and activities. The nurture group is an ideal setting for interactive, adult-led activities which will develop language and communication.

The following activities may be integrated into the foundation-stage classroom and possibly adapted for other age groups. By adding some of these activities to what is already planned, language and communication can be enhanced. The activities are designed so that all children can be included.

Arrival and Departure

This is a good time to teach social skills. Children can be encouraged to respond to greetings from adults and to each other.

Adult   Hello Maria

Child   Hello Mrs Jones

Adult   How are you today?

Child   I'm all right

Encourage children to greet one another and to initiate greeting.

Other questions naturally follow, for example:

How did you come to school today?
Who brought you? etc.

- Questions like these encourage thinking, understanding and language expression skills.

- Asking 'How' questions encourages the development of sequencing skills.

- Asking questions while a child is completing an activity, for example taking off their coat, can provide support and make the activity more meaningful.

Choosing time

Use a choice board. Using a picture symbol choice board will encourage children to make choices from several options. This will develop vocabulary (understanding and expression). It offers children who are withdrawn, with language delay or EAL the opportunity to participate in an activity.

Picture boards around the classroom can be used to encourage children with attention difficulties to follow through a choice that they have made.

Choosing time can be supported by asking children 'wh-' questions such as:

- What are you doing?

- What would you like?

- Who are you playing with?

- What is he/she doing?

- What happens next?

- Which is the smaller?

- When do you go to bed?

- Where should we put the bricks?

Asking these 'what', 'where', 'who', 'when' and 'which' questions, alongside 'how' questions, encourages children to answer using a longer sentence structure and further supports the development of cognitive skills. Making these open ended 'wh-' questions helps to encourage language development when closed questions (where the answer is yes or no or a 'right' answer) remove opportunities for development.

Choose target vocabulary related to a topic or a theme and ensure that there are opportunities to practise these words within the classroom. Write them up and display them around the classroom to remind adults of words which are a focus. The adults can model these words and encourage children to use them.

Set up sharing games and activities as part of choosing time. Adults should be available to support children with turn-taking or playing cooperatively.

The teacher can encourage children to say 'It is my/your turn'; 'May I have a turn?'; 'Your turn next'; 'I will go after you'. This models or gives children words that they can use for negotiation, a skill which they can use outside in the playground and with a wider group of people, to great effect.

Role play

Role play is a time to develop language skills. Imaginative play, negotiation, sharing and vocabulary extension all develop during role play. If a certain area of vocabulary is the focus this can be reinforced with symbolic support or by writing words down and placing them in the role-play area, for example in a café area using menu language.

Breakfast or snack time

Once children have settled in the nurture group they can be encouraged to make choices and to take an active role, although it is important to remember that the unfamiliar activities may need explaining before modelling, for example turn-taking may require the toast to be given out and children to wait until everyone is ready. As children make progress it will be possible to be less directive.

Begin with simple choices: 'Would you like jam or marmalade on your toast?'; 'Would you like milk or juice?'.

Managing more complex, open questions is another progression, e.g. 'What would you like to drink [or eat]?', etc.

Even the simplest, day-to-day activities need to be planned carefully for continuity and progression.

Modelling can follow when children may be 'helpers' and ask each other what they would like to eat or drink. This allows them to develop social and language skills in a group setting. Children like to help and this builds up their self-esteem.

Language around routines helps develop sequencing which is an essential pre-reading and early number skill, for example 'First wash your hands, dry them and then find a place to sit'. Similarly this language can support the daily management in the room, especially during transitions from activity to activity.

> - **It is understood that all behaviour is communication**
>
> - **Language as a vital means of communication**
>
> - **Children's learning is understood developmentally**
>
> - **The classroom offers a safe base**

Conclusion

Language and communication are essential aspects of the nurture group classroom. Keeping the relevant nurture group principles in mind enables the nurture group teacher in planning and the development of children's attachment.

The nurture group should be a rich context of language and communication between children and adults, particularly adults to adults and adults to children.

7

Creative development

Creativity is fundamental to successful learning. Being creative enables children to make connections between one area of learning and another and to extend their understanding. This area of learning includes art, music, dance, role play and imaginative play.

(*Curriculum Guidance for the Foundation Stage*, QCA/DfEE, 2000, p. 116).

Children in nurture groups should have the same opportunities to develop their creativity and imagination as other children in the school.

The importance of creativity and imagination

Bernadette Duffy (1998) identifies seven ways in which creativity and imagination are important in education. These include the following, which are most relevant to our work in nurture groups:

- The importance of creativity and imagination for the child, not just for the future but here and now, for communication, self-expression, understanding, discovering meaning, solving problems, self-esteem.

- The importance of representation: children need to represent their experiences, feelings and ideas in order to preserve them and share them with others, through symbolic representation they move from concrete to abstract thought.

- The contributions creativity and imagination make to other areas of learning: personal and social, language and literacy, mathematics, science and technology, history, geography, physical education. (See table 1.1 in Duffy, 1998, pp. 12 and 13 for more detail.)

According to Duffy:

Creativity and imagination come from the human ability to play and civilization rests on this ability. It is essential that we foster the human capacity for creativity and play, if we do not we will be left copying old ideas. Involvement in creativity and imaginative experiences should be for life.

(Duffy, 1998, p. 12)

Excellence in Schools (DfEE, 1997) and the response of the National Advisory Committee on Creative and Cultural Education titled *All Our Futures: Creativity, Culture and Education* (DfEE, 1999) as well as the Primary National Strategy *Excellence and Enjoyment* (DfES, 2003) all recognise that learning for the 21st century must take a broader view than just improving literacy and numeracy skills.

We need a broad, flexible and motivating curriculum that recognises the different talents of all children and delivers excellence for everyone.

(*All our Futures: Creativity, Culture and Education*, DfEE, 1999)

Creating an environment in the nurture group where creativity and imagination can flourish

The task of the nurture group is to recreate an environment in which children are able to relive missed early learning experiences.

The classic nurture group with its emphasis on learning through play provides a natural context for children to develop creatively and imaginatively.

Very young children or those (adults as well as children!) who have had little opportunity or encouragement for creative development may need to be introduced gently and systematically to the early stages of play that begin with sensory exploration.

They need:

- Time to explore and respond using all their senses: touch, sight, hearing, smell and – with care – taste.

- A trusted adult who can support, intervene, encourage and who recognises and values originality and expression.

- A range or resources to stimulate different ways of thinking.

- Attention to any special education needs and the appropriate provision and resources, for example for visual or hearing-impaired children.

- Sensitivity to religious or cultural beliefs.

Marjorie Boxall (2002) in her chapter on 'Earliest Learning Experiences', describes in detail how play was observed to develop in the children in the early nurture groups. In particular she notes that creative play develops because of the availability of toys and resources and 'the supportive presence and involvement of the adults.' (p. 97).

It is not enough for nurture group children to have access to the toys and materials, the presence of the adult is vital and nurture group principles must be followed at all times.

Further advice in *Curriculum Guidance for the Foundation Stage* (2000) on creative development, learning and teaching (pp. 116–19) holds good throughout the primary school and need not be limited to Early Years settings. It is recognised, however, that often nurture group children are older than those for whom the guidance has been written. For those older children the nurture group teacher will want to consider aspects of the National Curriculum for Key Stages 1 and 2, but although considering concepts at a higher level, there will be the need for play in discovering them. All children need to spend time with adults who are themselves creative and who understand and value creativity and imagination as well as having the necessary knowledge and skills.

Knowledge, skills and understanding

This section supports the idea concluded in the previous section that nurture group teachers need to explore a wide variety of concepts through play. The suggested aspects and concepts may be explored through art and design, music and dance, and drama. The section concludes with reflection on the Discovery Basket approach in supporting 'Responding to experiences' – part of the *Curriculum Guidance for the Foundation Stage*. It is recognised that many other foundation subjects of the National Curriculum could be considered here, but space does not permit this. Future publications will explore adaptation of the subjects and concepts in the National Curriculum to a play environment.

Earlier chapters in this book have shown that nurture groups, whatever the age of the children, may need to concentrate on helping all children confidently achieve the early learning goals for the foundation stage (considering the Nurture Curriculum, the Nurturing Curriculum and The National Curriculum). The foundation stage suggests four foci:

- Exploring media and materials;

- Imagination;

- Responding to experiences;

and

- Express and communicate their ideas, thoughts and feelings.

Exploring media and materials

Colour
Texture
Shape
Form
Space in two or three dimensions

Art and Design

There are eight elements to consider within art and design. Children need experiences, in two and three dimensional art, to explore and represent using these elements:

- Pattern – repetition of shape, colour and light

- Texture – characteristics or qualities of surface

- Colour – hue, intensity, saturation, brilliance, primary colours, secondary colours

- Line – a mark, stroke, strip, dash

- Tone – lightness or darkness, shade

- Shape – outline

- Form – 3D experience of shape

- Space – area between shapes

All children should have the opportunity to experience two dimensional drawing, painting, printing, textiles and photography. In three dimensional activities children should experience construction, sculpting and modelling. Ideas are included in the table over the page. All these experiences offer opportunity to develop skills and abilities which will also be transferable to other disciplines. These form the third column of the table.

Two Dimensional

Drawing

Using a wide range of graphic and mark-making tools such as fingers, pencils, charcoal, computer

Surfaces: different textures and sizes of paper and card, chalkboards, computer screens, permissible walls and pavements

Subject matter: physical attributes, abstract concepts such as sound of a drum, recording movement

Investigating marks and the quality of lines, rubbings

Painting

Hues – primary and secondary, shades – pastel, dark, light

Sorts of paints – powder, block, natural dyes, ready and self-mixed

Techniques for applying paint – fingers, feet, selection of brushes, marbling, spraying, splashing, stencilling

Surfaces – paper and card of different sizes and texture

Printing

Using a wide range of objects – hands, natural and found materials, raised and embossed

Surfaces – paper, card, fabric, walls, clay

Forms – patterns (repeated and single), natural shapes, manufactured

Textiles

Techniques – plaiting, twisting, winding, sewing, dyeing, appliqué, printing, knitting

Cloths and threads – wool, canvas, Hessian, linen, string, cotton, printed materials, raffia, grasses, twigs

Photography

Range of cameras

Light sources and images; light-sensitive paper

Three dimensional

Construction – forming representations by fitting together using a wide range of:

Commercial and found materials – bricks, blocks, Lego, wood

Different ways of joining – using glue gun, gluing, tying, knotting, hammering, threading, looping, nailing, screwing, brass fastening, paper clipping, stapling, treasury-tagging, binding, interlocking pieces

Different ways of parting – cutting, tearing, sawing, punching holes

Different forms – mobiles, collages, models, books

Sculpting – forming representations by chiselling or carving using a wide range of:

Materials – wood, salt, sand, stone

Tools – hands, fingers, cutlery, saws, commercial tools

Techniques – carving, hammering

Modelling – working plastic materials into shape using a wide range of:

Materials – papier mache, clay, dough

Tools – hands, fingers, cutlery, commercial tools

Techniques – moulding, pinching, scooping, flattening, rolling, thumbing, squeezing, attaching, wedging

Skills and Abilities

Observation

Interpretation

Estimation

Measurement

Experimentation

Investigation

Prediction

Problem solving

Recollection

Recording

Fine manipulation

Gross motor skills

Correct use of tools, equipment and materials

Communication

Hand and eye coordination

Tidiness

Coordination of eyes, hands and fingers

Carefulness

Accuracy

Safety

Joining

Parting

Comparing size, shape, height

Estimating volume

Balancing

These Skills and Abilities may be developed across all curriculum subject areas as well as within Art and Design

Imagination

Use imagination in art and design (see above)
Music
Dance
Imaginative and role play
Stories

Music and Dance

As art and design have eight elements, the National Curriculum identifies seven elements of music. The statutory guidance identifies what must be taught, but not how, and it is here that play and exploration of the elements of music and the three aspects of dance (weight, space and time) will support vulnerable children's development. The table on pages 62–63 gives some ideas for the Nurture Group Curriculum.

By introducing music and dance as a natural response to different stimuli children will have opportunity to explore aspects of the curriculum through play. There is evidence that the acquisition of musical knowledge and skills is developmental in nature. But within the disciplines themselves there is a developmental nature – composing and creating (formal aspects that might not be appropriate in the nurture group) require a building up of ideas. Unless children have had opportunity to play with the elements they will not have the skills and knowledge necessary to access the curriculum. While this is true of all children, it is particularly true of nurture group children.

Drama

The National Curriculum doesn't identify drama as a separate subject but sees it within English for Key Stages 1 and 2 but aspects of the foundation stage are often lost when children move into Key Stage 1. As with music and dance, these vulnerable children need to continue to explore imaginative and role play and experience stories. So, importantly, continue reading to the children – everyone loves a good story, but also consider telling (as opposed to reading) a story. Use props to help such as puppets or story boards so children can retell the story. While every nurture group should have a homely environment, it will be important to have a home corner for 'acting out'. With older children other imaginative play corners which should reflect familiar settings (e.g. hospital, doctors, etc.). Consider having a 'prop box' – a dressing up box for older children – so children can explore themes and ideas (being old, a baby, a mother or father etc.).

It may be necessary to model your expectations of children using imagination. Be aware of going completely into role and upsetting the security of the nurture group. Whilst becoming a Victorian teacher may be appropriate for the age of children you have, it may be disconcerting for children in the nurture group. You need to be consistent in your behaviour. But you should be working alongside children, playing in the home corner, imaginative play area, with instruments, dancing and using the puppets. Through these activities relationships can develop strong bonds, not unlike that of the mother and child.

Music	Dance

Rhymes and rhythm – elements, skills and knowledge developed through the two media:
- Cooperation, listening and internalising sound
- Time and space (dance)
- Duration, dynamics, tempo (music)

Music	Dance
Finger rhymes – including toddler favourites like 'round and round the garden . . .'	**Simple country dancing** – use well-known movements like circle clockwise for 8, anticlockwise for 8, doh-se-doh, skip/promenade with partner, girls/boys to middle and out, stars clockwise etc.
Copy my pattern – clap a simple pattern and children copy it (keep short – 4, 6 or 8 beats is usually best) but move the copying on so that pace is good.	**Follow my leader** – traditional game, but great fun.
Simon Says – like the traditional game, but Simon Says when you hear this pattern (clap it) don't copy it.	**Mirroring** – working in pairs with one of the pair leading and other copying as if in a mirror.
Name games – clap the pattern or rhythm of your name (first and family) and have children repeat it. Individuals can lead with their names. Used for registration.	

Singing – elements, skills and knowledge developed through the two media:
- Listening, internalising sound, concentration
- Space and weight (dance)
- Pitch, duration, dynamics, tempo, texture (music)

Music	Dance
Favourite songs – build up a repertoire of children's favourites and to remind yourself have them up high on the classroom walls.	**Move about while singing** – use the whole body in response to songs, not just the voice.
Nursery rhymes – although children may feel too easy this can be a great history topic.	**Movement songs** – use songs such as Head, Shoulders, Knees and Toes; Okey Kokey; Brown Girl in a Ring; In and Out the Dusty Bluebells; Oranges and Lemons; The Big Ship Sails, etc.
Pass the sound – Pass a sound around a group (e.g. 'buzzz' or 'whoosh') Pass more than one and see what happens when the two meet!	
Harmony work – play with just singing notes together, then introduce simple tunes that go together, e.g. Are you sleeping, Brother John and Three Blind Mice.	

Music **Dance**

Using instruments and pre-recorded music – elements, skills and knowledge developed through the two media:

- Cooperation, listening and internalising sound, managing materials and resources, concentrating, sharing
- Time, weight and space (dance)
- Pitch, duration, dynamics, tempo, texture, timbre, structure (music)

Display – music table, area or corner – display areas have different functions:

- Giving information e.g. about some class of musical instruments
- Sharing work done by children with others
- Being an interactive or working display – one which you expect children to touch and use (tip: in the classroom have a cloth which you can throw over an interactive display if you do not want the children to interact at certain times).

Pass the instrument – pass an instrument around a group and encourage children to play it in a different way (introduce musical ideas – e.g. loudly, softly, fast, rhythms etc.).

Instrument games – reorganise games suggested earlier (e.g. name game) so that children play rhythms on instruments.

Play music tapes and CDs – try introducing children to your tastes in music by playing your favourite.

Music tapes and CDs – respond in any way moving high, low, widely, using hands, feet, body on the floor, individually, with a partner, in a whole group (i.e. country dancing)

Ribbons, balloons, parachute – introduce different objects to move with. Explore height and space.

Discover types of dance – using different music will open the world of dance – waltz, ballet, tap etc. Allow children to share experiences from out of school time.

Responding to experiences

Children should be encouraged to respond in a variety of ways to what they see, hear, smell, touch and feel. For many in the nurture group this may seem awkward as the children may be chronologically older. The Discovery Basket may facilitate this.

The Discovery Basket

Commercially produced resources do not generally meet the needs of nurture group children particularly in the early stages. Just as young children in the home often show a preference for playing with a cardboard box or items from the kitchen cupboard so nurture children have been observed to spend a long time – sometimes up to an hour at a time – exploring the contents of the Discovery Basket. For children who are often described by their teachers as having poor concentration, this is remarkable.

The Discovery Basket was adapted by nurture group teachers from Elinor Goldschmied's Treasure Basket (Goldschmied, 1994). It is a total curriculum resource from the pre-foundation stage at developmentally from about eight months and with possibility for progression and continuity through other Key Stages. It offers possibility for all stages of play:

- Solitary, sensory exploration
- Playing alongside
- Experimentation
- Repetition
- Investigation
- Exploration
- Sharing
- Choosing
- Waiting
- Cooperative play with another
- Turn-taking – alternating
- Cooperative play with a small group
- Turn-taking with others

Concepts and motor and manipulation skills are developed and the foundations of maths, science, art, music, role play/drama are laid. Similarly, personal, social and emotional development, communication and language from pre-verbal to higher National Curriculum levels are integral.

A resource to encourage early play, concept, language and motor skills development

In many nurture groups there are at least one or two and sometimes more children whose concentration is very limited and who are unable to play. These children need opportunities to learn again to play from the very beginning but before they can do that they need to be held, cuddled and to build an attachment with the adult. Very often their social and emotional development can be identified as between birth and eight months.

What next?

Once trust is established it is time to begin the process of letting go or separation. In considering babies who are securely attached from the beginning the first signs of this may be seen from about four months onwards. As with the secure baby, nurture children need this warm, encouraging and welcome response to their growing sense of themselves as individuals. But the leap we expect in school in terms of autonomy and level of play is often too great and difficulties ensue. Some children may cling out of fear of the next step because of earlier bad experiences or perhaps they erupt immediately into the temper tantrum stage and become frustrated and angry.

The Discovery Basket is a resource that allows and supports this process of moving on to take place as naturally as possible. It aims to replicate the level of play that is provided for naturally in the well-organised home.

It is a good sized rush or wicker basket which contains a range of natural objects and small items in a wide range of different natural materials which are in every day use. They should be easily available and of the kind which might be found in a reasonably well-organised home and its surroundings and which give a young child opportunities for play.

The basket should be substantial enough for a child to lean against without it collapsing. In addition to natural objects such as conkers, fire cones, sponge, loofah, apple, orange etc., items made of wood, metal, paper and card, leather, fabric should also be included. Plastic should be avoided as most children are familiar with it and its only attribute apart from shape and size is colour.

> **Health and safety is important and items should be checked regularly for cleanliness and safety and replaced as necessary.**

Where to begin: solitary play

Sit the child on the carpet between the adult's feet facing outwards. Put the basket with a selection of items in it within reach and allow the child to explore, responding to expressed interest but not initiating conversation; perhaps naming items and drawing attention to their attributes as they are held up for you to see; smiling and commenting and chatting to your helper and other children nearby but not engaging in formal language development – that will come later. It would be a distraction now from the pre-verbal level of sensory exploration that is the focus.

Protect the child's space from others as a mother would protect a baby from boisterous toddlers.

Over the next few days gradually introduce new items. No more than one or two at a time, to maintain interest.

Observe and record the child's attention span, notice physical characteristics such as posture, hand grip, coordination and any language that is used. This is an excellent assessment opportunity for language and you may consider, for example is it monosyllabic or are sentences used, nouns only or adjectives and verbs as well?

This is a precious opportunity for observation and learning about this stage of development both for the benefit of this particular child but also for the adult's own learning. It will inform the adult about the child's level of development, enabling other appropriate activities to be planned.

It is important that the child is allowed to stay with the activity as long as is needed. This is a vital step in learning to attend and to concentrate as well discover, through this sensory exploration, fundamental information about the objects. This process cannot be rushed. As with all early learning this is the child's work and all future learning depends on it.

Introducing cooperative play

As you observe closely, you will notice that the child begins to manipulate the items and explore their function rather than simply their attributes. For example, a round object may roll away and others may be looked for that will also roll; or two objects may be placed one on another and all the objects then explored to see if they may also be built up.

The child may now be ready to play alongside another child. Babies at this stage have been observed to be aware of one another and seen to show signs of early social interaction. The children can be encouraged to find particular items such as those that can be placed on each other and built, placed one inside another, will roll, etc. Observe the actions they perform and particularly any interaction and conversation between them or the absence of it.

At a later stage a third child may be introduced. Simple, small group games are now possible provided the children are able to cope with them.

Games to play

'Who can find . . . ?' games which include a richness of language further support this early play. These may include:

- Name the attribute, for example size – large, small; colour – black, red; will roll; can be built up, etc.

- Name the object. Progress to playing memory games, for example 'I went to market and bought a . . .'

- Two, three or four . . .

'Who can find . . . ?' games can then be extended with finding a chosen object described – by name, by attribute, by colour, by size, by position, by the sound it makes, etc. Or by hiding an object and giving clues as to its position, attributes, etc.

Language development grows naturally from this type of activity, just as it does with young children in the home; it is rooted in the child's development and widening experience. The language development can cross into other subject areas such as mathematics with the inclusion of number, size and quantitative language, art with colour, texture and form language, science language, etc. This cross curricular role of language is important in developing children's literacy.

Other learning

New concepts are explored and formed which underpin future mathematics and science, knowledge and understanding of the world (humanities); creative development in the use of the senses and imagination; further exploring colour, texture and form in art; sounds and duration in music.

The activities which can be devised from using the Discovery Basket will link into the Stepping Stones of the *Curriculum Guidance for the Foundation Stage* (QCA/DfEE, 2000). They may then be developed into a Nurture/Nurturing Curriculum to meet the earliest learning needs of most children.

Working with older children

The Discovery Basket was used successfully with children in KS2 in the early days of nurture groups. It can be introduced with a more explicit subject in mind related to an aspect of the curriculum but ensuring that the opportunities for social and emotional learning have a high priority. For example, a range of items around a science focus such as materials, items which will encourage imaginative writing on a particular theme.

Express and communicate their ideas, thoughts and feelings

Using a widening range of materials
Suitable tools
Imaginative and role play
Movement
Designing and making

Many aspects of the previous three foci apply to this section too. Just the list of areas to be considered could repeat many of the activities already suggested, but it is important to consider the nature of **communication** within these and the potential for children to **express** themselves rather than **Explore, Imagine** or **Respond**.

Using a widening range of materials
Suitable tools
Designing and making

As children explore and use materials they will be ready to transfer their developing skills to more media in art and design & technology. It will be important to explore tools and materials that may require more fine motor skills (e.g. use of craft knives and wood).

Imaginative and role play

Examples within the Drama section already identified apply here, but also development of the home corner is important in the nurture group. Nurture children need many opportunities to act out family relationships, and, as with good early years practice there may be opportunity to extend the home corner perhaps by taking it outside. Older children in particular enjoy the opportunity to play imaginary games outside chasing ghosts and spectres, and developing fantasy ideas.

Movement

Movement is an early development within dance and music. Young children naturally use their whole body in response to music, but older children are not necessarily encouraged to explore movement in this way. Opportunities to work in larger spaces such as a school hall or outside in the playground or on a field with music or poetry may mean children can explore movement ideas further.

Conclusion

Creative development is vitally important, even more for nurture group children. Activities which are planned as described within the curriculum – the Discovery Basket, music, dance, drama, art and design – enable open-ended learning through play and exploration which further allows the earliest levels of development to be achieved with children who would normally have passed these levels. The opportunity to revisit early development is crucial for nurture group children. This chapter has attempted to consider the ways that these opportunities can be realised.

8

Monitoring, assessment, recording, reporting and accountability

All teachers have professional responsibilities for monitoring, assessment, recording, reporting and accountability. Nurture group teachers are no exception and in some aspects they may have more responsibility than a mainstream class teacher. The degree to which they are responsible will largely depend on their status and seniority in the school and school organisation.

This section focuses on these responsibilities from the perspective of the nurture group teacher rather than from a nurture teacher's wider involvement in the work of the school as a whole.

Monitoring

The nurture group teacher will have an important role in monitoring the behaviour and achievement of:

- potential members of the nurture group;

- children selected for the nurture group;

- children who are reintegrating.

Potential members of the nurture group

These will be children who have been identified and referred by class teachers or they may be children who are recognised by the nurture teacher or others as in need of nurture group support but class teachers may not be aware of their needs.

Quiet, withdrawn, non-participating children may be overlooked or even seen to be 'good' although they have hidden developmental needs that may lead to difficulties in the future.

Children who do not conform to the school or teacher's expectations may be referred to the nurture group but careful selection according to the school's agreed criteria is essential for success.

Schools often devise their own checklists for preliminary screening before using the Boxall Profile to identify needs more precisely. A copy of one such checklist is included here (see Appendix 2, pp. 80–82).

Not all children will benefit from the nurture group placement nor will the group as a whole 'work' if intake into the group is not carefully managed. The group needs to be balanced with no more than two-thirds acting-out children. Gender and ethnicity are also important considerations and should reflect the school population overall.

It is usual for the children to be from a single age phase i.e. KS1, KS2 or KS3. As the focus in the group is on levels of development rather than chronology a cross-phase group may, with careful curriculum planning, be possible.

Children who are not admitted to the group will be kept under review. An established nurture group is often a source of advice and a model for good nurturing practice and many children in mainstream classes also benefit from the presence of a group within the school. It may be that a place will become available later or a part-time place or occasional visit can be arranged to offer a degree of support and also, importantly, respite for a class.

Where it is decided that a child will on no account be admitted to the group alternative provision will need to be made to meet her/his SEN. In such cases the record of the observations and assessment using the Boxall Profile will be vital evidence for obtaining support or in finding an appropriate placement.

Children selected for the nurture group

These children become the nurture teacher's immediate priority in collaboration with the class teacher. As it is usual for them to remain on the register of their base class the class teacher will keep an overview of their attainment and progress in relation to the rest of the class/year group but s/he will rely on the nurture teacher for information about progress while in the nurture group.

The class teacher will need to know attainment levels and progress in the National Curriculum subjects. Progress in PSED may still fall within the pre-foundation stage Nurture Curriculum or indicate SEN in the Nurturing Curriculum, that is, children may be working in an earlier Key Stage.

The relationship between the class teacher and nurture teacher is crucial and the respective roles and responsibilities need to be clearly established. Some schools find it helpful to draw up 'An Understanding' between the class teacher and nurture group staff. In the London Borough of Enfield this is now authority-wide practice. A copy of Enfield's document is included (see Appendix 3, p. 83).

Children who are reintegrating

Re-integration is a dynamic process over a period of some weeks or even months. It will require close liaison and monitoring from both class and nurture teachers to ensure success particularly at times of transition or stress.

It is not unusual for the nurture group staff to maintain an interest in the child's progress at an informal level for the remainder of their time in the school – and even beyond! This is an important aspect of the extended professional role of the nurture teacher who continues to 'hold' the children in mind long after they cease to be her immediate responsibility.

A variety of checklists for readiness for reintegration exist in nurture groups and LAs across the country. A sample is included here (see Appendix 4, pp. 84–89).

Assessment and record keeping

Formal procedures

Most schools have well developed record-keeping systems for National Curriculum attainment and progress and SAT scores. Where this is the case the nurture teacher will follow the existing procedures as far as they are helpful in providing a profile of the child, although often more frequent assessments are made and recorded for areas of particular difficulty as in the case of any child with SEN. P scales will be used if appropriate for assessment in English, maths and science or the Stepping Stones of the foundation stage may be appropriate.

Where the school does not have adequate procedures for nurture group children it is suggested that a diary record is kept supplemented with samples of work that are clearly named and dated. Some schools use strategies such as post-its or notebooks to record on the spot significant observations or achievements for later entry into the diary record.

In addition to National Curriculum records there is a need to record progress in the Nurture Curriculum i.e. pre-foundation stage PSED. The tool available for nurture groups for this area of learning is the Boxall Profile. Training in using the Boxall Profile is an essential part of the four-day certificate course and it should be used according to the guidance in *The Boxall Profile: Handbook for Teachers* (Bennathan and Boxall, 1998).

Data to assist with completion of the Boxall profile is also best recorded in diary form on a daily basis, recording observations of behaviour and progress through the developmental stages by all involved with the child. Some schools devise their own proforma to record quantitive data, for example incidence of temper tantrums, fights or, for non-communicating children, initiating contact, touch, etc. This can be especially helpful for particularly challenging children where slow progress may go almost undetected. Just one fewer temper tantrum or fight a week may indicate the beginning of an improvement and be an encouragement to the staff and a spur to the child. A sample proforma is included here (see Appendix 5, pp. 90–91).

Informal procedures

In addition to the daily diary record contributing to the requirement on teachers to assess and record progress, informal record keeping has value in its own right. Some nurture teachers make detailed child studies that are invaluable for reaching a deeper understanding of children's needs and how we can best meet these needs in the mainstream school. Most of the insights, links to theory and the good practice that we have now, has come about from these indepth studies and reflection on them. When used as material for discussion among a group of teachers or educational psychologists they are invaluable.

This process of observation and recording has the additional benefit of assisting nurture teachers to detach themselves from the often highly charged emotional engagement with a particularly challenging child and enabling them to respond more positively than would otherwise be possible.

Reporting and accountability

Oral reporting to parents

Nurture teachers will contribute to parent consultations and open evenings alongside the class teacher wherever possible.

In addition, they will normally have their own informal and probably more flexible systems for keeping parents informed about their child's progress in learning and behaviour on a more frequent basis than most class teachers. Often this is daily, although hard to reach parents will need special arrangements to be made. Marjorie Boxall makes some suggestions (2002, pp. 164–5) based on previous practice but most schools develop their own and these are an important feature of the nurturing school.

Annual written report to parents

Annual written reports to parents are a statutory requirement for schools. The class teacher has responsibility for reporting on children registered in her/his class but nurture teachers will contribute to the report on the areas of learning for which they have been responsible, particularly PSED progress in the nurture group.

Evaluation

All schools are accountable for the resources provided to them and there is a responsibility on governors, local authorities and funding bodies to ensure value for money. A nurture teacher will be expected to keep statistical data for this purpose. Some local authorities such has the London Borough of Enfield have established procedures for collecting data and publishing their evaluations. This is good practice that is now being followed more widely. Samples from Enfield schools are shown in Appendix 6, p. 92.

Appendices

Appendix 1: 'Earliest learning: a summary chart'
(reprinted by permission of Sage Publications Ltd from Marjorie Boxall,
Nurture Groups in School, Copyright © Marjorie Boxall, 2002)

EARLY NURTURE

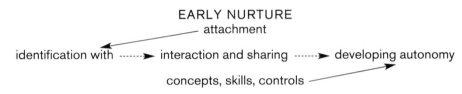

THE CONTEXT OF EARLY CHILDHOOD EXPERIENCES

The baby/toddler in the home	Re-created structures in the nurture group
The baby is emotionally and physically attached from the beginning, is physically dependent and needs protection.	Close physical proximity in the home area in a domestic setting facilitates emotional and physical attachment.
His experiences are determined by his developmental level (mobility, vision, interest, attention), and mother's intuitive response to his needs.	T/A (teacher/assistant) select basic experiences, and control them. They emphasize developmentally relevant features and direct the child's attention to these.
His waking day is short, slow-moving, broken up by rest and routines. There is a clear time structure. His physical needs determine the rhythm of the day.	The day is broken up by slow-moving interludes and routines. Everything is taken slowly, and there is a clear time structure.
The mother provides simple, restricted, repetitive routines and consistent management from the beginning, and manageable learning experiences through appropriate play materials and developmentally relevant interaction.	The teacher establishes routines, emphasizes order and routine; ensures much repetition. She achieves/conveys her behavioural expectations by clear prohibitions and limits. Toys and activities are developmentally relevant, and the adults' language and interaction is appropriate for this level.

The situation is made appropriate for an earlier developmental level; simpler, more immediate, more routinized, more protected. Restrictions and constraints provide clarity of experience and focus the child's attention; he engages at this level, his attention is held and there is much repetition. Basic experiences and attachment to the adult are consolidated. The child experiences satisfaction and approval, and attachment to the adult is strengthened. Routine gives security and he anticipates with confidence and pleasure

Growth promoting patterns are established.

THE CONTENT OF EARLY CHILDHOOD EXPERIENCES

'Mother's lap'
Attachment and proximity: earliest learning

Food, comfort, holding close; consistent care and support.	Food, comfort, close physical contact; consistent care and support.
Cradling, rocking; sensory exploration; touch in communication.	Cradling, rocking; sensory exploration; touch in communication.
Intense concentration on mother's eyes and face. She communicates her mood/feelings in her face/voice; spontaneous exaggerates her response.	T/A draws children's attention to her eyes and face. Makes and establishes eye contact. They deliberately exaggerate their facial expression, and tone of voice.
Closeness; intimate interplay; shared feelings/satisfaction. Mother's verbal accompaniment reflects pleasure, and child's loveableness and value. She makes frequent positive acknowledgements of her child.	There is closeness; intimate interplay and shared feelings/satisfaction. The T/A's verbal accompaniment reflects pleasure, and child's loveableness and value. They make frequent positive acknowledgement of each child.
She has age-appropriate expectations; accepts asocial behaviour but controls events and provides manageable constraints and alternatives.	T/As have developmentally appropriate expectations. They tolerate asocial behaviour but give purposeful direction, control events and provide manageable constraints and alternatives.

'Mother's lap'
Attachment and proximity: earliest learning

The foundations of trust, security, positive mood and identity are built through continuing support and shared basic satisfactions in the context of adult–child emotional attachment and physical proximity. Feelings are communicated and shared, and there is close identification and empathy, the one with the other, and an empathetic response to subtle non-verbal signals. Shared experiences, registered in language, leads to an understanding of basic attributes and properties of materials, and of objects and their relationships, and cause and effect.

and

'Mother's knee'

The child has already internalised the security that comes from attachment to a reliable, attentive, comforting parent and this security is reinforced through the continuing repetition of the simple routines of his daily life. These become a familiar and meaningful sequence of events, and through them the child gains a sense that the world about him is stable, orderly and predictable. In the course of physical maturation in an appropriate environment he has acquired basic competencies. He has also experienced adequately consistent management of his behaviour, achieved and conveyed by explicit setting of boundaries.

From this secure base the parents help the child to personal autonomy through a complex process of letting go and bringing back. He is 'let go' into experiences that the parents control and ensure are manageable, and where support is provided when needed, and he is 'brought back' to the security of close contact with the parents when the situation is overwhelming and he can no longer cope. Because the parent is sensitively involved and intervenes when necessary, new experiences are manageable and the child is able to assimilate and consolidate them.

Letting go and bringing back: developing autonomy

'Mother's day'

Child does things with mother, or with mother nearby. There is frequent contact and reassurance and expression of pleasure and approval.	Children do things with T/A or with T/A near; are collected together frequently with calmness and reassurance and eye contact is re-established.
Child shows spontaneously arising need for 'transitional objects' providing comfort, support, control.	The T/A make 'transitional objects' available to provide comfort, support, control, and may introduce them.

S/he gives attention to simple experiment and repetitive play and of own accord persists at this level. There is much experiment and repetition.

S/he engages in simple investigation and exploration, and because this is limited by his/her physical development and mother's intervention, frustration is tolerable.

Mother gives help with basic skills, procedures, and provides information, suggestions, ideas.

Mother helps/intervenes when necessary; often plays with child for mutual enjoyment. They share experiences, learn together. Mother responds with pleasure to each new achievement.

Relationships are individual. Mother intuitively identifies child/object/task by name, and provides a developmentally relevant running commentary.

Child's development is gradual, and simple experience, in the course of physical maturation, come before complex ones. Mother prepares her child for new experiences; anticipates and describes events and feelings in simple language.

Sharing, choosing, come in manageable stages. There is enough play space. Mother supports/controls co-operative play with other children; anticipates problems, averts, intervenes; identifies with and shares child's feelings.

Child needs/demands order. Mother meets own and child's need for order by providing routine and orderliness. She involves her child in orderly routines such as tidying up, sorting out and putting away.

Mother provides simple consistent basic training. Makes clear her expectations, demonstrates. Her approval/disapproval is immediate and evident. She gives help and reminders when necessary. Her verbal commentary and reinforcement at this early level are simple and basic and reflect the achievement.

They introduce, demonstrate, and share early play, with experiment and repetition. Support, encouragement, pressure help them to persist at their developmental level.

Teacher selects basic experiences for investigation and exploration; She controls and directs these, anticipates and avoids unmanageable situations; diverts attention. Unnecessary frustration is reduced.

T/A gives help with basic skills, procedures, provides information, suggestions, ideas.

T/A helps/intervenes when necessary; often plays with child for mutual enjoyment. They share experiences, learn together. T/A gives immediate praise for each small gain.

Requests/instructions to the children are at first individual, never general; child/object/task specifically named, and there is continuing verbalization.

Everything in incremental stages, simple before complex; situation structured; essentials highlighted; complex instructions broken down. Detailed preparation for each new experience; feelings anticipated and described.

Need to share is deliberately limited at first (enough for everyone). Grabbing is controlled. Sharing/choosing are built into manageable stages; Play space is respected. Co-operative work/play is not expected, but is encouraged, introduced, controlled. T/A anticipates problems, averts, intervenes; identifies with and shares child's feelings.

Routines structure the day. Sorting out, and tidying up and putting away are stressed. T/A shows them what to do.

Simple, consistent, unremitting basic training. T/A make their expectations clear and constantly stress them, with demonstration when appropriate. They give immediate and evident approval/disapproval and help and reminders when necessary. Their verbal commentary and reinforcement reflect child's level and achievement.

The situation is made manageable and support is there when needed; new experiences are assimilated and consolidated, and the child explores with purpose and confidence. He becomes personally better organized and realizes that he has some control over his environment. He learns to give and take and control his own behaviour, and makes constructive relationships that provide satisfaction and extend his horizons. He can now manage on his own for limited periods in a familiar situation and will soon be able to function without direct help in a bigger group.

The foundations of the child's autonomy are becoming established.

Appendix 2: Screening checklist

Name _____   DOB _____

Class/setting   _____

Date of observation _____

Situation in which observed

**Enfield Early Years
Social Inclusion**

Number in group   _____

Siblings (eldest first) _____

_____

_____

Length of time in setting _____

Attendance pattern

Any other factors (please tick)

    Vision impairment

    Hearing impairment

    Motor co-ordination

    Medical problem

    Limited understanding of English

Nature of concern

    EBD

    GLD

    SpLD

    Comm/Lang

    Other

General comment

Appendix 3: An understanding between class teacher and nurture group staff

An Understanding between class teacher and Nurture Group staff

_ _ _ _ _ _ _ _ _ _ _ _ _ _ _ will be joining the Nurture Group.

Enfield Early Years Social Inclusion

I understand I need to:–

1   Welcome the child in the morning, register him/her and keep him/her until he/she is collected by Nurture Group staff.

2   Endeavour to include the child in all school activities – such as assemblies, PE, Games Golden Time, visits, parties, etc.

3   Endeavour to develop a positive relationship with the child.

4   Welcome the child and accommodate him/her when joining the class at the end of each day.

5   Send home reading books regularly and also any other appropriate homework.

6   Liaise with Nurture Group staff re: information, messages, behaviour, etc.

7   Agree on a programme of re-integration into mainstream class.

8   Attend review meetings with Nurture Group staff, Education Psychologist, SENCO and parents where appropriate.

We (the Nurture Group staff) will:–

1   Organise and maintain a suitable learning environment in accordance with Nurture Group principles.

2   Work in a focussed and creative way on helping the child meet his/her targets on his/her IEP.

3   Develop a positive relationship with the child.

4   Keep careful records – daily.

5   Maintain on-going assessment and review of the child's work and progress.

6   Endeavour to develop a good relationship with parents and carers.

7   Liaise with class teacher regularly.

8   Attend review meetings with class teachers, Education Psychologist, SENCO and parents where appropriate.

9   Be available to parents, class teachers etc.

Signed . . . . Class Teacher   Date . . . .

Signed . . . . Nurture Group   Date . . . .

Signed . . . . Nurture Group   Date . . . .

Appendix 4: Readiness for reintegration

Self-control and management of behaviour				
Can accept discipline without argument or sulking	1	2	3	4
Can arrive in classroom and settle down quietly and appropriately	1	2	3	4
Does not leave the room without permission	1	2	3	4
Can accept changes to plans or disappointment with an even temper	1	2	3	4
Shows some self-discipline when others try to encourage deviation	1	2	3	4
Is aware of normal sound levels and can be reminded of them and respond appropriately	1	2	3	4
Does not seek confrontation during unstructured times, e.g. break	1	2	3	4
Behaves in socially acceptable manner in public, e.g. outings	1	2	3	4
Can maintain appropriate levels of behaviour when the class routine is disrupted	1	2	3	4
Will abide by the accepted rules of an organised group game	1	2	3	4
Behaves appropriately in all areas of the school building	1	2	3	4
Goes to and stays in designated areas when requested e.g. playground, hall, etc.	1	2	3	4
Controls emotions appropriately when faced with difficulties, e.g. does not fight, strike out immediately, run away and hide or become excessively withdrawn	1	2	3	4
			Score	/52

1 = rarely fulfils the criteria

2 = can occasionally fulfil this criteria

3 = frequently fulfils this criteria

4 = criteria met 90% of the time

Source: Adapted from Rebecca Doyle (2001), used with permission.

Appendix 4: Readiness for reintegration (cont.)

Social skills				
Can cope with large numbers of people	1	2	3	4
Can accept that teacher time needs to be shared	1	2	3	4
Can ask a question and wait for the answer	1	2	3	4
Can take turns in question and answer session	1	2	3	4
Has appropriate communication skills, e.g. talking, asking questions and listening	1	2	3	4
Can work alongside others in a group situation without disruption	1	2	3	4
Interacts and plays in a positive way with peers	1	2	3	4
Apologises without reminder	1	2	3	4
Asks permission to use objects belonging to another person	1	2	3	4
Shows empathy for and comforts playmates in distress	1	2	3	4
Chooses own friends and maintains reciprocal friendships	1	2	3	4
Makes and accepts normal physical contact with others	1	2	3	4
Accomodates other children who ask to join an activity	1	2	3	4
Is self-reliant in managing own hygiene and basic needs	1	2	3	4
Shows genuine interest in the news or activities of another child	1	2	3	4
Contributes actively to play with two or more children	1	2	3	4
Shows variation in the roles undertaken during co-operative play, e.g. is not always the role of the dominant character, etc.	1	2	3	4
Engages in appropriate conversation with another child, exchanging information and using appropriate dialogue	1	2	3	4
Addresses adults and children appropriately by name with eye contact	1	2	3	4
Shares legitimately required equipment with another pupil	1	2	3	4
	Score			/80

Appendix 4: Readiness for reintegration (cont.)

Self-awareness and confidence				
Willing to ask for help	1	2	3	4
Can accept responsibility for his/her actions without denial	1	2	3	4
Can acknowledge own problems and is willing to discuss them	1	2	3	4
Can risk failure	1	2	3	4
States feelings about self, e.g. angry, happy, sad	1	2	3	4
Maintains appropriate eye contact	1	2	3	4
Contributes to class discussions	1	2	3	4
Participates in group work, making constructive suggestions and adapting ideas	1	2	3	4
Responds appropriately to stories, identifying the characters, e.g. funny, kind, bad, scary	1	2	3	4
Participates in large class activities, e.g. dance, role plays, performances	1	2	3	4
Accepts public praise and congratulation appropriately, e.g. when good work is shown to peers, etc.	1	2	3	4
Shows pride in achievements and presentation of work	1	2	3	4
Has esteem for self	1	2	3	4
	Score			/52

Appendix 4: Readiness for reintegration (cont.)

Skills for learning				
Can work alone without constant attention for brief periods	1	2	3	4
Can listen to explanations and instructions and attempt to act on them	1	2	3	4
Understands the structure within the day	1	2	3	4
Understands the roles of the teacher and other adults in the school	1	2	3	4
Understands the structure of discipline – what happens if he/she does not conform to playground rules etc.	1	2	3	4
Understands that there are different places for lessons other than the classroom, e.g. library, PE hall, etc. and behaves appropriately	1	2	3	4
Can constructively use unstructured time in the classroom	1	2	3	4
Can organise him/herself if help is not immediately available	1	2	3	4
Responds appropriately to personal request from teacher	1	2	3	4
Will work alongside another pupil without attempting any distractions	1	2	3	4
Can organise the materials needed for a task and clear them away appropriately	1	2	3	4
Shows appropriate levels of curiosity when changes to the normal routine are observed	1	2	3	4
Reading and numeracy up to a level that can be coped with in a mainstream classroom given reasonable support	1	2	3	4
Shows a willingness to improve own literacy and numeracy	1	2	3	4
Can read sufficiently well to understand basic instructions needed for completion of tasks	1	2	3	4
Has developed some self-help strategies (at own level), e.g. using reference materials such as word banks	1	2	3	4
Does not get up and wander around classroom without purpose	1	2	3	4
Needs a mainstream curriculum	1	2	3	4
Does not get impatient if help is not immediately forthcoming	1	2	3	4
Is willing to try to complete a task independently	1	2	3	4
Pays attention to class discussions and instructions	1	2	3	4
	Score			/84

Appendix 4: Readiness for reintegration (cont.)

Approach to learning				
Is prepared to work in lessons	1	2	3	4
Uses appropriate language and gestures	1	2	3	4
Wants to be reintegrated	1	2	3	4
Has parental support	1	2	3	4
Is courteous, and shows a positive attitude towards staff	1	2	3	4
Can show a positive interest in lessons	1	2	3	4
Treats school property with care	1	2	3	4
Listens with interest to class explanations	1	2	3	4
Can accept disappointments e.g. when not chosen to participate in an activity	1	2	3	4
Will sit appropriately without causing disturbance in both class and general school areas on request	1	2	3	4
Shows a sense of humour	1	2	3	4
	Score			/44

Appendix 4: Readiness for reintegration (cont.)

Record of progress towards reintegration

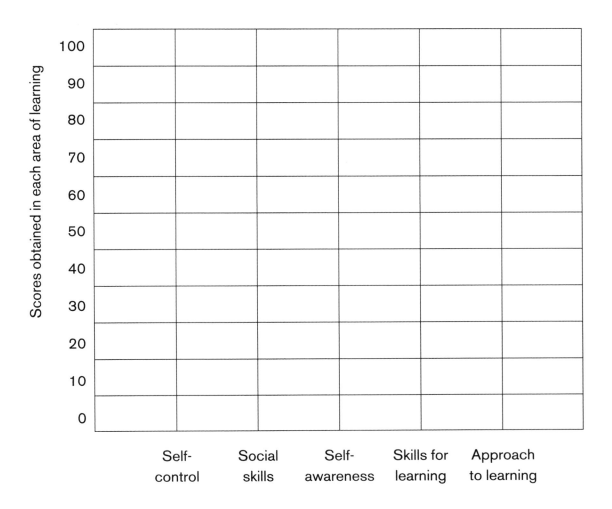

Areas of Learning

Key: enter date and colour of pen used for ease of identification

Date:		Date:		Date:		Date:	
Date:		Date:		Date:		Date:	

Appendix 5: Possible proforma for a child's Individual Record Sheet for one half term

Name of Child:
Entry to group:
School:

		Week 1	Week 2	Week 3	Week 4	Week 5	Week 6	Week 7
1 Need for cuddles, cradling, baby play etc								
2 Dependence on NGT/NGA for support	a							
a) comfort; b) control	b							
3 Response to	a							
a) approval; b)disapproval	b							
4 Need for transitional objects for support	a							
a) comfort; b) control	b							
5 Interest shown in teacher and helper	a							
a) physical interest; b) seeks information	b							
6 Development of child's self-image	a							
a) physical interest; b) seeks information	b							
7 Greed for	a							
a) food; b) toys	b							
8 Interest in bodily functions								
9 Interest in violence								
10 Sex interest								
Sex play (*see key)								
11 Temper tantrums								
a) frequency; b) severity (**see key)								
12 Fights								
a) frequency; b) severity (**see key)								
13 Aggressive swearing								
14 Sulks, pouts, clenches fists etc								
15 Behaviour problems								
a) outings; b) playground/dinner-time								
16 Intervention of another person necessary								
a) in class; b) out of class								
17 Attitude to families:								
Neutral or not shown O								
Positive + or ++								
Negative – or – – (***see key)								
18 Comes in late or truants								
Attendance /10								

Key:

0 Not observed
+ Somewhat
++ Marked

Sex interest & play*
+++ excited;
sophisticated

Fights & temper
tantrums**
+++ berserk
Please also indicate
time taken to subside

Attitude to family***
0 Neutral or not
shown
+, – Somewhat +ve
or –ve
++,– – Markedly +ve
or –ve

Note
Please note that the
weeks indicated are
those of the half term
rather than those in
the Nurture Group.

It will help to add the
actual date to these.

Appendix 5: Possible proforma for a child's Individual Record Sheet for one half term (cont.)

Code A Level of play
1 Fidgets, sucks, messes, bangs
2 Looks on
3 Treats playthings aggressively
4 Solitary play, repetitive
5 Solitary play, imaginative
6 Plays alongside another child
7 Joins with others in common activity
8 Organised and imaginative play, e.g. families, making a boat
9 Formal games

Code B Level of conversation
1 Repeats sounds
2 Talks to self
3 Addresses remarks to other person; no response expected
4 Alternates with another child, each following his own theme
5 Adapts conversation to other child
6 Exchange of information
7 Conversation

Code C Attention Span
(the longest continuous attention shown)

Less than	1 minute	1
	5 minutes	5
	10 minutes	10
	15 minutes	15
	30 minutes	30
More than	30 minutes	30+

	1st week	2nd week	3rd week	4th week	5th week	6th week	7th week
19 Level of play (see code A)							
Play materials used							
Attention Span (see code C)							
20 Level of conversation (see code B)							
Content							
Attention Span							
21 Nature of academic and formal creative work (describe)							
Attention Span							
22 Involvement with other classes:							
Amount –							
Response –							
23 Does any part of the school day particularly evoke fights and temper tantrums?							
24 Any reason for mental improvement or deterioration (?home, ?school)							
25 Have new characteristics from the Development Profile appeared?							
26 Any other comments							

Source: Adapted from proforma used in ILEA nurture groups 1973.

Appendix 6: Review of data

Review of data always serves to demonstrate that nurture groups are excellent value for money. Below are charts summarizing the successes of two Enfield nurture groups.

School A

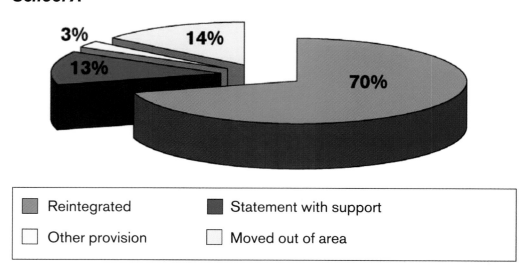

■ Reintegrated	■ Statement with support
□ Other provision	□ Moved out of area

School B

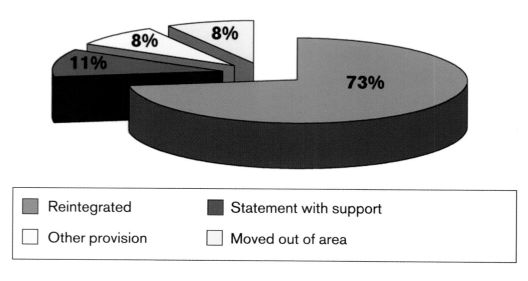

■ Reintegrated	■ Statement with support
□ Other provision	□ Moved out of area

Collection and evaluation of data in Enfield provided the evidence base to secure the money from the LA to extend the provision of funding by the borough for nurture groups. This will allow for the development of one new nurture group each year 2005–2008. This is full funding for a full-time group with a teacher and TA in charge. They will then be funded to attend the four-day course at the Institute of Education prior to the establishment of the group.

Bibliography and Resources

Bennathan, M. and Boxall, M. (1998) *The Boxall Profile: Handbook for Teachers*. AWCEBD. Available from The Nurture Group Network.

Bennathan, M. and Boxall, M. (2000) *Effective Intervention in Primary Schools*. London: David Fulton. Available from The Nurture Group Network.

Boxall, M. (2002) *Nurture Groups in School: Principles and Practice.* London: Paul Chapman. Available from The Nurture Group Network.

DfEE (1997) *Excellence for All Children: Meeting Special Educational Needs*. London: HMSO.

DfEE/QCA (1999) *The National Curriculum*. Available online at http://www.nc.uk.net (accessed 12/04/06).

DfES (2001) *Inclusive Schooling*. Available online at http://www.teachernet.gov.uk/_doc/4621/InclusiveSchooling.pdf (accessed 12/04/06).

DfES (2003) *Excellence and Enjoyment: A Strategy for Primary Schools*. London: DfES publications. Available to download at http://www.standards.dfes.gov.uk/primary/publications/literacy/63553/ (accessed 12/04/06).

DfES (2003) *Every Child Matters*. Government green paper.

DfES (2004) *Every Child Matters: Change for Children*.

Dowling, M. (2000) *Young Children's Personal, Social and Emotional Development*. London: Paul Chapman.

Duffy, B. (1998) *Supporting Creativity and Imagination in the Early Years*. Buckingham Philadelphia: Open University Press.

EYSI (Enfield Early Years Social Inclusion Project) *The Developmental Stages of Language and Communication*.

Gerhardt, S. (2004) *Why Love Matters: How Affection Shapes a Baby's Brain.* Hove and New York: Brunner-Routledge.

Goldschmied, E.(1987) Babies at Work (video). London: National children's Bureau.

Goldschmied, E. and Jackson, S. (1994*) People under Three: Young Children in Day Care.* London: Routledge.

Lucas, S. (forthcoming) *The Discovery Basket: A Curriculum Resource for Nurture Group Children.*

McNeil, F. (1999*) Brain Research and Learning – An Introduction.* SIN Research Matters, Institute of Education University of London.

NACCCE report (1999) *All Our Futures: Creativity, Culture and Education.* DfEE.

QCA/DfEE (2000) *Curriculum Guidance for the Foundation Stage.* Ref: QCA/00/587.

Useful documents

Accessible Schools: Planning to Increase Access to Schools for Disabled Pupils (DfES 2002). Ref: LEA/0168/2002.

Disability Rights Commission: Code of Practice for Schools (Disability Rights Commission, 2002).

Inclusive Schooling: Children with Special Educational Needs (DfES 2001). Ref: DfES 0774/2001.

Planning, Teaching and Assessing the Curriculum for Pupils with Learning Difficulties (QCA 2001).

Special Educational Needs Code of Practice (DfES 2001). Ref: DfES 0581/2001.

SEN Toolkit (DfES 2001). Ref: DfES 0558/2001.

Supporting Pupils with Special Educational Needs in the Literacy Hour (DfES 2000). Ref: DfES 0101/2000.

Towards the National Curriculum for Mathematics: examples of what pupils with special educational needs should be able to do at each P level (DfES 2001). Ref. DfES 0637/2001.

Websites

Inclusion

http://www.qca.org.uk/6166.html

http://www.nc.uk.net/inclusion.html

http://www.nc.uk.net/nc_resources/html/inclusion.shtml

http://inclusion.ngfl.gov.uk

General

http://www.everychildmatters.gov.uk

http://www.ican.org.uk – helping children to communicate

http://www.literacytrust.org.uk

http://www.ourschools.org.uk

http://www.nc.uk.net

http://www.standards.dfes.gov.uk

http://www.tda.gov.uk

http://www.teachernet.gov.uk/teachers

Useful Addresses

EYSI (Early Years Social Inclusion)
4 Pitfield Way
Enfield, EN3 5BW

Nurture Group Network
004 Spitfire Studios
63–71 Collier Street, London N1 9BE

School of Early Childhood and Primary Education (ECPE)
Institute of Education
University of London
20 Bedford Way
London, WC1H 0AL

QCA Orderline
P.O. Box 29, Norwich, NR3 1GN
Tel: 08700 60 60 15, Fax: 08700 60 60 17
Email: orderline@qca.org.uk

Index

Achievement 12
Art and design 57
Assessment 5, 27, 33, 43,
    71, 74
Attachment 11, 42

Behaviour 14, 22, 41, 42
Bereavement 15
Boundaries 11
Boxall Profile 6, 14, 20, 30,
    33, 72, 74
Breakfast 50

Change 15
Choosing 49
Classic model 35, 55
Class teachers 6, 17, 27, 33
Communication 10, 13, 37,
    41, 44, 46
Commentary 13
Conversation 13
Coordination 10
Creativity 53
Cross phase groups 36

Dance 60, 62, 63
Differentiation 22, 28
Discovery basket 64
Drama 60

Educational psychologists 6
Effective learning environment
    21, 40
Enfield (London Borough) 6
Equal opportunities 21
Evaluation 75
Every Child Matters 5, 7, 29
Eye contact 12, 46

Feelings 13

Food 11
Full time groups 35

'Good enough' parent 29

Head teachers 6

Imagination 53, 60
Individual Education Plan (IEP)
    14, 27
Individual Learning Plan 14,
    27, 28, 31, 33, 34
Inclusion 5, 17, 26

Language acquisition 41
Language development 12,
    37, 42, 44, 48
Learning mentors 6
Literacy 45

Monitoring 71
Motor development 10
Music 44, 60, 62

National Curriculum 5, 7, 17,
    31, 35
Neuroscience 6, 32
Non verbal communication 14
Nurture Curriculum 7, 11, 20,
    28, 29, 30, 35
Nurture group assistant 11
Nurture work 6
Nurturing Curriculum 5, 30,
    35

Observation 14
Off site visits 15

Parents 15, 75
Part time groups 36

P scales 7, 20
Physical contact 14
Planning 27
Play 10, 11, 13, 55, 56, 61,
    66
Pre foundation stage 5
Programmes of study 17, 31

Reading 22, 41
Reintegration 15, 73
Recording 14, 71, 74
Role play 20, 50
Relationships 6, 11, 14, 35,
    36, 61
Remembering 12
Routines 11, 15, 21, 37, 51

Selection 22, 72
Separation 15
Singing 12, 62
Speech and language delay
    13
Structure 11

Teachers 6
Teacher absence 15
Teaching assistants 6, 35
Team work 36
Theory and practice 5
Training 7
Training and Development
    Agency 31
Transitional objects 15
Transitions 15
Turn taking 47, 50

Visitors 15
Voice 12

Wave 3 7, 35